G000099261

THE LAND CALLED 'DELLES'

*THE HISTORY OF THE ELIS DAVID AND LITTLE
ALMSHOUSES OF CROYDON*

BY SUE TURNBULL

A RESIDENT

ISBN 0-9549133-0-2

© Sue Turnbull, 2005. All rights reserved

Published by: Sue Turnbull, The Clerk's Office

Elis David Almshouse, Duppas Hill Terrace, Croydon, Surrey CRO 4BT

Printed by Advanced Print Services, Coulsdon, Surrey.

LIST OF CONTENTS

IN MEMORY OF
ELIAS, MATILDA AND ELENA DAVY

AND DEDICATED TO
THE PEOPLE OF CROYDON

FOREWORD

It is most appropriate that there should be a historical link between one of Croydon's oldest charitable foundations and the Mercers' Company, the premier City of London Livery Company. Elias Davy was a prominent Mercer of his day, who founded his almshouses in 1447, inspired by the example of his fellow Mercer, Richard Whittington. Over the centuries, the Mercers' Company has maintained a link with the Elis David Almshouses (as they came to be known), now under the auspices of The Croydon Almshouse Charities. Today my Mercer colleague, Christopher Clementi, represents the Mercers' Company as a Trustee and in writing this foreword I have benefited from his close relationship with the modern charity. It is an integral part of the function of the Mercers' Company today to manage benefactions founded around Davy's time. Indeed, our records date back to 1348, and I am pleased that our archives have been of considerable help to Sue Turnbull in researching her History, which has taken her on a fascinating journey through time.

Sue, a nurse by training, has, in her retirement, taught herself how to go about detailed historical research. She has produced the first definitive history of the Croydon almshouses, originally built on land bequeathed by Davy, and has studied a number of original sources never before consulted, even by local historians working before her. I am aware that she has put in a vast amount of time, work and dedication into producing her History, which has been a labour of love. She has also set up a history room in the almshouses, where she is a resident, and gives regular local history talks.

Whilst Sue looks back through the centuries, I am delighted to know that today the Croydon Almshouse Charities are as active and innovative as at any time in their history. The trustees are currently redeveloping the Elis David Almshouses in an imaginative scheme, which will provide much improved accommodation to meet the expectations of the 21st century. This is no easy task to achieve, whilst at the same time endeavouring to minimise inconvenience for the residents. The Trustees, through an associated charity, are also an important grant making body providing financial support to a wide variety of different charities operating in the London Borough of Croydon.

It is a long time since the Master and Wardens of the Mercers' Company were personally responsible for 'overseeing' the Elis David Almshouses, but nevertheless I warmly recommend Sue's History of these almshouses.

Charles C Scott
Master of the Mercers' Company
November 2004

INTRODUCTION

High on Duppas Hill Terrace, overlooking Croydon's fire station, is a six-storey red brick building bearing the name 'Elis David Almshouses'. It was here that, in 1997, I was fortunate enough to be given accommodation and the opportunity in my retirement of researching its history - an adventure that took me through nearly six hundred years of the history of Croydon, its parish church and people.

Today's almshouse, built in 1974 and officially opened on 25 March 1975 by Princess Alexandra, combined the original Elis David Almshouse, Church Street, with the Henry Smith Almshouse, Scarbrook Road (the 1896 replacement for the original Little Almshouse, Church Street).

It is owned and managed by the Croydon Almshouse Charities, a twentieth-century amalgamation of individual benefactions both great and small; the greatest of all being the original gift to Croydon of lands and an endowed almshouse by Elias Davy, Citizen and Mercer of London, in 1447.

Despite the hazards of fire, human destruction and error, and Acts of God, numerous records have survived for me to track down in a variety of locations and this is but a brief account of my findings.

I am well aware that the present almshouse is a monument to those legions of people who gave something of themselves to make it all possible; and it is a matter of some pride that Croydon's oldest charitable foundation is alive and well in the twenty- first century!

Sue Turnbull

ACKNOWLEDGEMENTS

I would like to express my thanks to the following for their assistance and encouragement:

Noel Hepworth, Chairman, the Trustees of the Croydon Almshouse Charities and Bill Rymer, Clerk to the Trustees.

The Master and Wardens of the Mercers' Company. Ursula Carlyle, the Mercers' Company Curator and Archivist. Christopher Clementi, Mercer and Trustee of the Croydon Almshouse Charities.

Steve Roud, Chris Bennett, Christine Corner, Grace Woutersz, Margaret Mumford and the staff of Croydon Local Studies Library and Archives.

Melanie Barber and the staff of Lambeth Palace Library. John Gent, Brian Lancaster, Dr. Ron Cox and Ken Woodhams of the Croydon Natural History and Scientific Society. Stella Howlett, Manager, and the staff and residents of the Elis David Almshouse. Freddie Percy, Archivist, Whitgift Foundation. Canon Colin J. Luke Boswell, Vicar of Croydon. Maj.Gen. A. de C. L. Leask, CB CBE, Director, the Almshouse Association. Dr. T. Harper Smith of the Acton Local History Society. David Shakespeare of J.B. Shakespeare, Graham Reeves of E. Reeves and Else Churchill of the Society of Genealogists. John Coulter, Linda Goulding, Dorothy Huggett, Valerie Barnes, Andrew Graham, Janice and Derek Gerrard, Sue Bevan, Yvonne Walker, Tom Rogers, John Bird, Jonathan Bates, Geremy

Butler, Barbara Fitch and Dr. A. Fitch of Stockenden, Hilary Marshall for transcription of Elias Davy's purchase of land record and codicil of will and Joyce Kent for translation of Elias Davy's will. I am indebted to the late Clarence Paget for the use of his notebooks.

I should also like to thank Anthea Snoussi and my sister, Margaret Hawkes, for invaluable practical help.

ABBREVIATIONS

BL	British Library
CHC	Charity Commissioners
CLRO	Corporation of London Record Office
CLSLA	Croydon Local Studies Library and Archives
GL	Guildhall Library
LPL	Lambeth Palace Library
MCA	Mercers' Company Archives
TNA	The National Archives
SRO	Suffolk Record Office

ILLUSTRATIONS

By courtesy of the Mercers' Company: C1, C2, C4, 4, 5, 22

By courtesy of the Museum of London: 2 (IT 1283), 8 (IT 1308)

By permission of the British Library: 3. (Royal 17B XLVII f 133v-134)

By permission of the National Portrait Gallery, London: 10

By courtesy of Southwark Local Studies Library: 1

By courtesy of Croydon Local Studies Library and Archives: 11, 12, 13, 14, 15, 16, 17, 23, 25, 26, 28, 31

By courtesy of John Gent: 21, 24

Reproduced by kind permission of the *Croydon Advertiser* (Trinity Mirror Group): 34

By courtesy of John Bird: 7

By kind permission of Dr. and Mrs. A. Fitch: C3

Other illustrations were supplied by the author.

Cover design by Jonathan Bates

CHAPTER ONE: SETTING THE SCENE

Medieval Croydon

By the end of the Middle Ages Croydon was a thriving country town that had grown up around its parish church of Saxon origin dedicated to St. John the Baptist - an indication of the nearness of water. The church was surrounded by the trout-filled streams and tributaries of the river Wandle, the several sources of which rose in the higher ground towards the present High Street. The river Bourne flowed through the South Mead - today's Southbridge Road - and along Old Town to join the Wandle; in one place its tributary looped to form an area known as Bog Island, today's Salem Place.

Habitation had formalised along Old Town amongst the marshes and mud, which precipitated the problems that forced development onto higher ground in the area we know as Surrey Street. The adjoining Middle Row also disappeared under a modern building scheme on the site of what would later become Grants Department Store.

Croydon parish was vast: about 10,000 acres and 36 miles in circumference. It was bounded by Lambeth and Streatham in the north; Penge, Beckenham, West Wickham and Addington in the east; Addington, Sanderstead and Coulsdon in the south; and Beddington and Mitcham in the west.

Throughout the parish was a web of churchways (footpaths) leading from its outer boundaries to the church; the present-day High Street was then a bridle-path through fields in the early stages of residential development. Croydon was known as a place of beauty with its woods, park, fields and rivers.

These were feudal days, and the town was also known for its manor house situated next to the church. From before the Domesday survey, the Lord of the Manor was the Archbishop of Canterbury, and his lands included smaller manors such as Waddon, Norbury (including Bensham and Whitehorse), Haling, Croham and Coombe.

There was also an area of land called Rectory Manor, or the 'Bermondsey Hold' as it belonged to the Abbey of St. Saviour, Bermondsey. This was triangular in shape and bounded by Church Street, Crown Hill, North End, Handcross Road, down to the marshland at Pitlake north of the church.

Duppas Hill, which in later years would become famous for rare wild flowers, sported the Lord of the Manor's much-hated dove houses (the birds fed on grain as quickly as it was cast to the ground, creating a major frustration for the desperate peasant). Over and around it were the routes to Waddon.

Croydonians worked from dawn to dusk, mostly on the land, and life was dictated by the demands of the agricultural year. As elsewhere, a crop rotation was followed involving wheat, oats, barley and legumes. Croydon also produced the Archbishop's crop of rye. In the northern part of the parish was the Great North Wood where the Croydon Colliers producing charcoal for London achieved notoriety. There were also traders, craftsmen and innkeepers, with weekly markets since 1276 and three fairs a year, one of which was held in the Fair Field every September 21 and 22 from 1314 until 1868. Croydonians go to the same site for entertainment today.

Croydon was 10 miles from London and the route – much travelled by merchants, pilgrims, gentry and the rich and famous visitors to the Archbishop's Manor House and their retinues - passed along Handcross (now Handcroft) Road and London Road, through Streatham, Brixton and on to London Bridge. The journey was fraught with danger from marshland, brigands (later known as highwaymen) and other hazards. Croydon became a handy stop-off point on the London trade route (a day's journey) and tenements and parcels of land were sometimes leased for the storage of goods by members of the City Livery Companies. The southern route passed through Old Town and on to Godstone and the coast.

The Archbishops held a chain of manor houses between Lambeth and Canterbury, travelled with large retinues, and entertained visitors for both pleasure and ecclesiastical affairs – the latter being conducted wherever the Archbishop happened to be at the time and not delegated elsewhere until after the Reformation.

The Croydon manor house would have been in constant use for local administration, such as collection of rents from the Archbishop's tenants, and as a court for both ecclesiastical and civil matters. The strictly observed way of life was dictated by church and manorial customs. The town of Croydon was contained within four crosses: the Hand Cross (at the junction of Church Street and Lower Church Street), the Stay or Stake Cross (at the junction of Wellesley Road and George Street), another at the junction of High Street and Lower Coombe Road and the fourth at the junction of Duppas Hill Road and Old Town. Copyholders and freeholders living within these crosses were excused payment of certain dues to the Lord of the Manor.

In 1437, a list of services to be performed by the Archbishop's tenants was compiled by Robert Crull, Reeve of Croydon. It contains such items as the number of days to be worked ploughing for him, preparing his fields for crops, harvesting, mowing meadows, providing chickens at Christmas, eggs at Easter and so on.

In addition to obligations to the Lord of the Manor were the payment of tithes to rectors, vicars and monasteries. The great tithes consisted of corn and hay and the small tithes of livestock, wool and some crops. Croydon parish supported both a rector and a vicar, the rector receiving the larger amount although performing fewer duties- a bone of contention in later years. The payment of tithes became unpopular and controversial as the years went by.

Pivotal to the life of every parishioner, rich or poor, was the parish church where the major events of family life took place: baptisms (ideally carried out on the day of birth or as near to it as possible), marriages and funerals. In addition, masses were celebrated daily and Evensong in the afternoons. Sunday Services usually consisted of Matins at about 6 or 7am, Parochial or High Mass at 9 or 10am followed by a procession with the sprinkling of Holy Water and Evensong or Vespers at 2 or 3pm. Attendance at all services was compulsory. The Sunday sermon had its own importance both as a means of religious instruction and also - at a time when very few could read or write - in the communication of local affairs.

Other sacraments included Confirmation, Penance (obligatory at least once a year), and Extreme Unction at the point of death. Following childbirth came purification and blessing with the Churching of Women. The church bells were an important means of general communication and the ringing of the Angelus began the day at 4 or 6am, and ended it at 8 or 9pm.

Life was hard and there was little respite for the aged and sick, especially those with no family to support them. There was little understanding of disease, much superstition, cruelty, violence and insecurity. The arrival of Christianity had brought religious communities to this country providing alms of food, clothing, hospitality and money, education and medicine. Basic healthcare was undertaken by monks - usually away from their monasteries in hospitals or Lazar Houses for those with infectious diseases. This eventually led to the almshouse movement (and non-monastic hospitals) endowed by benefactors of all kinds. These were religiously based institutions with a daily life centred on prayer; their wardens were usually priests. Healthcare for the elderly was rudimentary and based on superstition, with herbs offered as antidotes to poison and infections, mad-dog bite, gout, rashes and flea deterrent (a major problem). Pain was treated with herbs such as lavender. There was a high incidence of osteoarthritis, occupational injuries and tetanus. Honey was given for just about anything and red flannel worn to counteract 'the stone'. Wheat soup made from husks and herbs and other similar preparations were given to the elderly and very frail.

Finance for this, as well as support for the poor of the parish, was provided through the giving of alms and the bequeathing of legacies, usually administered by the parish priest and churchwardens. Giving money for this purpose was considered a duty and much effort was put into the provision of charities in order to redeem souls from purgatory - a fate feared by all. Chantry chapels were set up by the wealthy with endowments for a priest to pray for the soul of the donor. There were two such chapels in Croydon Parish Church, one dedicated to St. Mary and founded in 1358 by Sir Reginald de Cobham, and the St. Nicholas Chapel founded in 1440 by John Stafford (then Bishop of Bath and Wells) together with William Oliver, Vicar of Croydon.

William Oliver came from a wealthy Croydon family and he also founded an almshouse for eight poor people. From his property he had arranged for 18d to be paid weekly for 100 years to the almspeople and for maintenance of the building. The site of this almshouse is unknown but, as his intentions were greater than his wealth, it failed and fell into disrepair. He was sent to Fleet Prison in 1444, deeply in debt to many people including the Archbishop. Ironically, perhaps, he died in the Hospital of St. Katherine - an almshouse - next to the Tower of London.

In 1443/4 one Elias Davy, Citizen of London and member of the Mercers' Company, purchased the land called Delles, for £15, with its 'hegerews heges and diches and all other appurtenances... lying in the parishe of Croydon in the shire of Surrey' from Richard Crulle, Citizen of London and bowyer.[1] The Crulles were a Surrey family often found in the employ of the Archbishops. Richard resided chiefly in Southwark.

There has always been confusion about Elias Davy's name as it has often been mistranscribed and mistranslated, even during his own lifetime. It is, therefore, sad but not surprising that his almshouse became Elis David Almshouse. Elias Davy (the correct spelling) has been variously recorded as Elyas Davy, Elys Davy, Elys Davye, Ellis Davy, Elis Davie, and David Ellis.

The land called Delles was extremely marshy with the river Wandle running through it, and the record of purchase suggests that there were doubts as to its viability. By 1447, however, it had been drained and contained four cottages, an almshouse for seven poor people, gardens and orchards.

This area today lies in Church Street from the north wall of the Rose and Crown to the northern end of Reeves' Corner island. It originally extended further to the west across what is now the Roman Way.

---

[1] Land Purchase Record BL Royal 17B XLVII f133b

The Mercers' Company

Livery Companies developed from early guilds and fraternities formed to protect and promote their members in particular crafts and trades. The Mercers' Company, the premier livery company of the City of London, dates back to the 13th century although their first Charter was not granted until 1394. It was central to the development of trade and commerce and many members played important roles in the civic governance of the city.

Mercers were merchants dealing mainly in wool, linen and luxury fabrics. Their trade extended well beyond London and even abroad. Elias Davy, for example, traded in Bruges.

In 1425, the Company was granted a second Charter and common seal showing a maid's head. The origin of this could have been in commemoration of the Virgin Mary but is more likely to have been a favoured inn sign! The Mercers' Maiden has been the Company's symbol ever since.

Mercers have always been involved in charitable activities and today this is the Company's main concern.

The Company Hall is situated in Ironmonger Lane, on the site of the Hospital of St. Thomas of Acon, Cheapside, founded in 1220 by St. Thomas Becket's sister on the site of his birthplace. From 1347 the Mercers held their meetings in a room at the hospital and held their services in the hospital chapel until 1517-24, when the Company built their own chapel and the first Mercers' Hall with a frontage onto Cheapside itself. In 1538, following the dissolution of the hospital, the Company purchased all the buildings on condition that a church was maintained on the site - the only one in a livery hall.

1. Seal of Bermondsey Abbey. 15th Century

2. Alms Box. 15th Century

3. 17th Century copy of Elias Davy's Land Purchase Record

CHAPTER TWO: ELIAS DAVY, THE MAN

Elias Davy was born c.1384/5, in a place as yet unidentified. It is often assumed he was born in Croydon on the basis that his almshouse was founded there. This may, indeed, have been the case, but it was more likely he was born in the City of London. Wherever he spent his early years, it could be reasonably assumed that it was in a religious household.

Originally, it was intended that he should be apprenticed to William Hawe, a distinguished Mercer and Alderman of Bassieshaw in the City of London. It is likely that William Hawe became unwell and possibly died before this could happen, as he disappeared from the records. Elias was actually apprenticed to Thomas Fauconer in 1398 at the age of about 14, two years later than a 'Thomas Davy' who may well have been a close relation.

Thomas Fauconer was a man of some consequence. Born in Norfolk, he became a Master of the Mercers' Company five times, the first being the year that Elias Davy commenced his apprenticeship. He was master to 26 apprentices during his lifetime, Collector of Taxes, Sheriff (of London and Middlesex), Alderman from 1402 onwards, Mayor of London 1414-15, Member of Parliament for Cheap Ward six times, collector of customs and subsidies in Southampton 1405-1407 and Boston 1407-1409, collector of the wool custom London 1412-1416. He became very wealthy, investing in land and property in Coventry, Kent, Berkshire,

Hampshire in addition to London and Norfolk. On several occasions he lent money to the Crown and became one of London's benefactors. He had dealings in most English ports, having his own ships and developing overseas trade. On one occasion he lost a cargo worth £240 to Flemish pirates and the King personally intervened to award compensation.

He made various transactions with fellow Mercer, Richard Whittington, with whom he was a co-feoffee (trustee).

His civic career, although long and distinguished, was not without its troubles. He was fiercely anti-Lollard (the Lollards challenged the established practices and doctrines of the church and were seen as heretics). In 1416 he suffered ongoing problems with John Russell, woolmonger, John Eston, joiner, and Richard Anable, pewterer, following his orders to close Anable's business because of various offences committed against the custom of the City the previous year.

Further offences were committed by the three troublemakers, including false and malicious accusations against Thomas Fauconer for which John Russell was found guilty. This incited the three men to cause even more difficulties for Thomas Fauconer. They used violence and intimidation against two of his apprentices and one of his servants continuously from 1 June to 27 July 1416, so that they became too afraid to go about their business. One of these apprentices was also called John Eston. One record suggests that the sentence was deferred, another suggests punishment by pillory; but the three continued to cause trouble. Towards the end of the year John Russell disappeared, abandoning his business and apprentice.

Thomas Fauconer and his wife Philippa had two daughters, Katherine and Thomasina. At that time, girls, whose lives were controlled by their fathers and brothers, were betrothed and married at an early age, often to men much older than themselves and usually for reasons of financial or social advancement. Katherine must have been a girl of some spirit, for in a Record of Protestation (27 January 1417), she complains that she was betrothed before she was five-years-old to William Moleyns, son of William Moleyns, Knight, and wished to 'take me an husbonde after the lawe of God to my plesyng'.[2] The record is incomplete but her protest did her no good, for she was indeed married to William Moleyns in around May of the same year and died a young woman some time afterwards. Her sister married Sir John Graa.

Thomas Fauconer died in office as an alderman between 21 September and 9 November 1434.

Elias Davy's apprenticeship would have provided him with excellent opportunities for the advancement of his occupation. Being in Thomas Fauconer's household, his daily life would have involved contact with the wealthy and politically powerful men who were at the centre of London's commercial life.

He gained the Freedom of the City in 1405/6 at the age of 21 and launched what was to be a successful career, although he was never to hold office in the Mercers' Company. In 1409/10 he took on apprentice Nicholas Lacey for the standard fee of two shillings. He was at his most successful by 1433.

[2] Record of Protestation LPL Reg. Henry Chichele Vol. 4

He would have married his first wife, Matilda, whilst in his early twenties; sadly she died, most probably in childbirth for which there was a high mortality rate. Apart from the complexities of labour, medieval women were often anaemic due largely to a meat-free diet based on grain and honey. Menstruation exacerbated this anaemia, as did multiple pregnancies.

Matilda Davy was buried in the St. Mary Chapel of the Hospital Church of St. Thomas of Acon, and there is reference to her tomb in his will.

Elias Davy was married for a second time about 1412 to Elena Roos, widow of Mercer Richard Roos who had died in 1409. It would appear that Richard had been much older than Elena and she was not his first wife. He already had two sons, Richard and Thomas, the latter being apprenticed to Richard Whittington in 1391/2.

Richard Whittington was born of a wealthy family in Pauntley, Gloucestershire. He was apprenticed to a London Mercer, became a millionaire, was made three times Master of the Mercers' Company and four times Mayor of London. His great benefactions to the City included Whittington College, his almshouse for thirteen poor folk. His illustrious civic career included sitting on commissions (1414 and 1418) to seek out Lollards. He married Alice, daughter of Sir Ivo Fitzwarin, in later life, and she died nine years after the marriage.

Richard Whittington died in January 1423/4. Thomas Roos, with whom he had many dealings and who, with Thomas Fauconer, was a co-feoffee for his property in the parish of St. Michael, Paternoster, was at his bedside.

On 18 September 1414 Elias Davy was, with others unnamed, fined £80 for assault and affray on one John Eston. Exactly when and why this offence occurred is unknown and the surviving records are incomplete. 1414 was the year of Lollard riots and it is possible that Elias Davy, a deeply religious man following the orthodox practices of the church, became somehow caught up in them. It is also likely that the John Eston involved was one of the three troublemakers already mentioned in connection with Thomas Fauconer - for whom Elias Davy would have had considerable loyalty. If this was the case, the problems rumbled on for eighteen months.

Elias Davy lived in the parish of St. Michael Bassieshaw (the church he attended) near to London's Guildhall and not far from the Mercers' Hall. He held several tenements in the area and was busy expanding his business and leading the full life of a member of a Livery Company - fulfilling duties as a trustee of various properties and orphan children.

On marrying Elena he became responsible for her son by Richard Roos, also called Richard, who died before maturity. Elias and Elena had two children of their own, Margaret and Elias. The latter died in childhood but Margaret was married to John Derby, Citizen and draper, auditor, sheriff, and alderman of Candlewick Ward. Derby was successful in his business and traded extensively abroad, including Genoa. In 1439 he was granted the Farm of the Aulnage of cloth. Aulnagers were required to be financially secure and experts in clothmaking. Their duties included the inspection of all cloth before it could be sold and ensuring that the legal length was observed before it was sealed.

John and Margaret Derby had two sons, Elias and John, both of whom received personal bequests from their grandfather in his will. Margaret Derby died before her father; her husband married again - to Joanna, daughter of John and Alice Caldebek.

In 1444 John Derby was fined £50 for not removing a dead dog from his doorway and for 'using opprobrious language' to the Mayor, John Yonge.[3]

On 19 October 1454 he was discharged from aldermanry and the court passed a special resolution allowing him to continue to wear his gown 'to keep him warm in severe weather'.[4] He was to be treated with continued respect.

John Derby lived and worshipped in the parish of St. Dionis Bakchurch, Fenchurch Street. In 1450, he provided a chapel dedicated to St. John on the south side of the church. Unfortunately, this church was destroyed in the Great Fire of 1666. It was replaced in 1684 by one designed by Wren that was demolished in 1878. John Derby died in 1480 and, in accordance with his will dated 17 February 1478, he was buried in St. John's Chapel. He left land and tenements to the church, partly for the maintenance of two chantry chapels. These were for the souls of Margaret, his late wife, Joanna, his present wife, her parents, his parents and himself. In 1519 there was an inquiry by the Drapers' Company into the neglect of his legacy by the priest and churchwardens.

---

[3] *The Aldermen of the City of London.* Beaven.
[4] Ibid.

There is no mention of his sons in John Derby's will so it is likely that they had both predeceased him.

In 1436 Elias Davy was in dispute with John Burton, merchant of Norwich in Norfolk, over a transaction in Bruges. John Audeley, Elias Davy's factor and attorney, had acquired linen and other merchandise to the value of £30 for his master from John Burton, and had sent the bill dated 10 December 1435 to Elias Davy for payment by 14 March following. The bill was never paid despite repeated requests and the dispute was taken to court. After several hearings in 1437, Elias Davy was ordered to pay the £30 plus 20 shillings' damages. Mercantile disputes were common, but this appears to be the only time Elias Davy was the defendant.

In 1443/4, at the age of 58, he purchased the land called Delles in Croydon and made preparations for building his almshouse. He obtained a licence from Henry VI signed at Westminster on 25 December 1444 and letters patent from the Archbishop, John Stafford, and John Bromleigh, Abbot of Bermondsey. Much of the next ten years was spent closely supervising his project.

In 1452/3 he took out a 60-year lease on a manor at Acton from the Priory and Convent of Saint Bartholomew, West Smithfield. This was intended as an investment to pay for 'a suitable and honest chaplain to pray for my soul, the soul of my parents, my friends and benefactors and all the humble and faithful deceased, in the chapel of the Blessed Mary in the church of St. John, Croydon' as laid down in his will. It is probable that he and Elena were residing there at the time of his death for his will stated 'Where I now live'.

Elias Davy died on 4 December 1455 aged 70 and, in accordance with his wishes, was buried in the north wall of the St. Mary Chapel in Croydon Church in a railed, canopied altar tomb of Purbeck marble with brasses.

Elias Davy's will, dated 3 November 1455 with codicil of 22 November, and written in the ecclesiastical Latin of the day, named his executors as John Kirkby, Citizen and Mercer of London, William Fitzwater, gentleman, William Clow (or Clover), scribe and curate, John Martin, Citizen of London and Mercer and Thomas Chambers (otherwise Fowler). The latter lived in Croydon and held land at Addiscombe. William Fitzwater also held land at Addiscombe and properties in Croydon whilst William Clow features in a number of London and Croydon records. He also held lands and property in Addiscombe and Bensham.

To the church of St. Michael in Bassieshaw, he left 13 shillings and fourpence for the rector to pray for his soul and 20 shillings for the fabric of the church; also five silver marks for each of 40 poor parishioners of the parish of Bassieshaw.

To Croydon Church he left his missal, tabard and multicoloured vestments of silk brocade; and ten silver marks for the fabric of the church.

He left his wife Elena her 'rightful share' of his goods and chattels, as well as the jewellery, silver and household goods which belonged to her before marriage, together with £100.

He left his servant Ann (or Alice) Dilman 20 marks of silver and expressed a wish 'that she may live free from poverty in my almshouse', presumably in the next vacancy.

Both his grandchildren were left 40 shillings and some silver. He also left £40 and some personal effects to Idone, daughter of Henry and Joan Islep, on condition that she and all her lands and tenements 'remain under the management of my executors until she marries.' If she should marry without the approval of the executors the legacy was to be null and void.

Three properties with adjoining gardens in the parish of St. Michael Bassieshaw yielding rents of 30 shillings were left to the Mercers' Company, on condition that the wardens pray annually for his soul and 'the souls of all faithful and humble deceased' in their chapel near the tomb of Matilda. In addition he left 40 shillings for a communal supper for the Mercers to follow the prayers.

The manor at Acton has already been mentioned. Davy required his executors to 'provide for the guardians and paupers in my almshouse at Croydon...and their successors' from all his lands and tenements. The residue of all his goods then remaining was to be used for the upkeep of the highways between London and Croydon and for prayers for his soul 'to the honour of God and for my salvation.'

Each of his executors were left 100 shillings, apart from Thomas Chambers who would receive 40 shillings.

Elena Davy appears to have outlived her husband. The vestments left to Croydon Church were destroyed in the fire of 1867. The church of St. Michael Bassieshaw was burned down in the Great Fire of London in 1666, rebuilt in 1676 by Sir Christopher Wren, then demolished in 1899 when the foundations were damaged during clearance work in the crypt. The site was purchased by the City Corporation and the parish was joined to that of St. Thomas Jewry. Today a plaque marks the site.

In 1495 an Alice Barrett brought an action in Chancery against one John Barowe. She accused him of pretending that he 'was possessed of the property at Acton' with the intention of using the profits for other things than supporting a priest to pray for the soul of Elias Davy.[5] She also charged him with illegally removing a mass book, chalice and vestments ordained for the purpose. The outcome of this action is unknown.

[5] Early Chancery Proceedings 117/48.

4. One of only two surviving impressions of the first seal of the Mercers' Company granted by the charter of Henry VI of 14 February 1425.

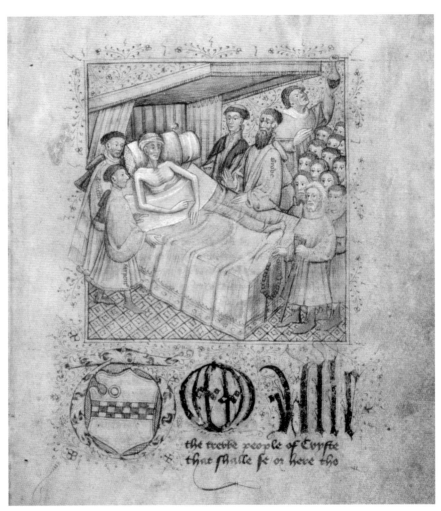

5. Richard Whittington on his deathbed in 1423, attributed to William Abell, pen and ink on vellum, from the first page of the *Whittington College Ordinances* of 1442.

6. Elis David Almshouse resident, John Aselford, at the site of the church of St. Michael, Bassieshaw, Basinghall Street, London, in 2000. Elias Davy lived nearby.

7. The present Vicar of Croydon, Canon Colin J. Luke Boswell, by the pillar that was erected on the site of Elias Davy's tomb in Croydon Parish Church following the fire of 1867. A reproduction plaque (Latin) can be seen on the wall behind him.
Photo: John Bird.

CHAPTER THREE: THE ELIS DAVID ALMSHOUSE CHURCH STREET

Elias Davy founded his almshouse in 'perpetuity'[6], an important concept as it was more usual to provide almshouses for a specified number of years, sometimes only a short period. His other intention was that it should be a kind of mini-monastery, a community of prayer and care. It was sometimes called a religious foundation on this basis. Equally important was the granting of a common seal and the required facility to increase the goods (land and property) belonging to the almshouse.

The Ordinances were signed on 27 April 1447, which is taken as the founding date. They were long and detailed with every provision made for long-term security. They were also, in places, word-for-word the same as those for the Whittington Almshouse, the management of which had been taken over by the Mercers' Company in 1443. This may well be an indication of Elias Davy's admiration for his fellow Mercer, but it could simply have been more a matter of practicality.

The almshouse was to accommodate seven poor people of either sex, one resident to be the Tutor with particular duties and responsibilities[7]. They were all to 'live in love and charity with one another', be 'meek of spirit, chaste of body', of 'good conversation' and 'destitute of temporal goods' by which they may 'competantly live'. They were expected to be honest, able, devout and to obey the requirement of the ordinances.[8]

---

[6] Taken from the Introduction to the Ordinances.
[7] In documents before the 20th century the inhabitants of the Elis David Almshouse were referred to as 'The Tutor and Poor People'. I have referred to them using the modern terminology of 'residents'.
[8] Ordinances of the Elis David Almshouse, 1447. Unless otherwise stated, all quotes in this chapter are taken from this document.

The governors of the almshouse were to be the vicar and churchwardens of Croydon Church and four of the 'most worthy men', householders and parishioners, resident within the town of Croydon.

The overseers were to be the Master and Wardens of the Mercers' Company; they were to visit annually to oversee the governance and to be paid their costs.

The tutor was to be appointed within 20 days of a vacancy by the governors. Other resident vacancies were to be filled within 15 days; applicants were to be resident within four miles of Croydon Church. In the event of more than one applicant, the residents were to hold an election in which the tutor was to have two votes. Residents were to have lived in Croydon for at least seven years, to be unable to earn their living, and to 'Have not wherof to sustain them with'.

During his lifetime Elias Davy was to be responsible for admissions and discharges, rules and governances. After his death this would become the tutor's responsibility.

The almshouse was endowed with £18 annually from the rent of the four cottages and farmland on the land called Delles. Fifteen pounds and twelve shillings was for the residents' weekly allowance of ten pence each and 12 pence for the tutor for 'Sustenance'. The remaining money was to be used for the maintenance of the almshouse.

Each resident was to have a room to himself in which to live and rest, to make no noise or disturbance, to be no trouble to his fellows, to live peacefully and quietly, occupying himself in praying and sleeping, to labour 'in body and hands to the laws and worship of Almighty God' and 'in profit' to the residents and the almshouse.

All residents were to be 'mighty and whole of body' especially women, and to minister unto their sick and feeble fellows giving whatever help was needed.

No madman, leper or any person with 'intolerable weakness' was to be admitted. Any resident who became so was to be 'put out lest he infect his fellows' and would have to go elsewhere. He would, however, continue receiving 10d every week for living expenses and necessities, and would still be counted as one of the number during his lifetime.

Residents were not to be out all night in Croydon or elsewhere without reasonable cause and the consent of the tutor and other residents. They were not to be drunk, gluttonous, troublemakers, haunters of taverns, or to 'walk or gaze in the open streets of Croydon by day or night', out of sight of the almshouse except to go to the church or churchyard. Offenders were to be 'corrected' by the tutor by the withdrawal of their allowance which was to be put into the common chest. A third offence would result in being expelled from the almshouse and the place given to someone else.

Any almshouse resident begging or asking for silver or any goods was to be expelled at once and no longer be 'of the fellowship'.

The tutor was not to be absent more than six days in the year without the permission of the governors and overseers; any absence had to be for a 'necessary cause in an honest place'. Other residents were not to be absent for more than one day without permission of the tutor, who was to appoint a deputy whenever he was going out of the almshouse.

The tutor and residents were to have a common chest in which to keep their common seal, charters, deeds, letters of licence and privileges, muniments, scripts, money and treasures. The chest was to be kept in a secret place in the almshouse. It had three locks and the three keys were kept by the tutor, the eldest fellow and another resident chosen by Elias Davy, and after his death by the tutor and residents. No man was to have all three keys; nothing was to be sealed without the advice of Elias Davy, and after his death the governors and overseers.

The tutor and residents were not to waste the goods belonging to the almshouse and all were to work to increase the goods and keep them safe. When a resident died he was to leave his possessions to the almshouse.

Any resident receiving an inheritance or other sum of three marks or more per annum was to leave the almshouse; for a lesser sum, half was to go into the chest or the resident had to leave.

The tutor had the responsibility of ensuring that the almshouse goods were properly administered, encouraging 'peace and charity' amongst his fellows, and of setting an example of 'cleanliness and virtue' in word and deed.

Every new tutor, within a month of admission, was to make an inventory of the common moveable goods, assisted by two of the most discreet residents. A report was to be given to the governors at the end of every year or at the change of a tutor so that everything could be accounted for.

After the death of Elias Davy the governors and overseers were to make statutes and ordinances to the increase of the almshouse and the welfare of the tutor and residents.

The residents were to attend daily every divine service in Croydon Church and to pray especially for the estates of the Sovereign Lord King with three Paternosters, three Aves and a Crede with a special recommendation of the founder to 'God and the Blessed Lady Maiden Mary'.

In addition, every resident, at other times of the day, to say three Sawters of Our Lady (i.e. three Ave Marias, 15 Paternosters, and three Credes) for the estate of the souls of the above, unless excused for reasons of feebleness.

Also, once a day at least, after High Mass and before Compline, to gather round the tomb of Elias Davy and say, for his soul and the souls of the above-mentioned, the Psalm de Profundis with all the versicles and orisonnes that belong; or, for those that could not, three Paternosters, three Aves and one Crede.

When this was done, the tutor and one of the eldest men of them all should say openly, in English, 'God have mercy on our Founder's soul and on all Christians and they that standeth shall answer "Amen" '.

The founder ordained that every year after his decease the tutor and residents should celebrate his 'Years Mynde' (anniversary) in Croydon Church. The vicar was to be paid 20d for this.

The residents were to wear overclothing of dark brown 'not staring neither blasing, and of easy price cloth, according to ther degree'.

The ordinances were to be read openly and clearly explained every quarter-year to the tutor and residents; it would have been very unlikely that the residents would have been able to read themselves. There was also to be a copy on permanent display in the almshouse.

The above is a very condensed version of the Ordinances, which contain a description establishing that the river Wandle ran past the north side of the almshouse building. To the south were the three cottages, gardens and orchards. North of the river was another cottage and farmland, all to be rented and the profits used for residents' allowances and maintenance of the almshouse. Roads lay to the east (towards the church) and north (to London). To the south lay the tenement 'of William Oliver, late vicar of Croydon' in which John Fauxwell 'nowe dwellith' .

The Mynde Day service would have been held on 4 December until the Reformation. It was resurrected in the year 2000 for the first time when 14 residents gathered in the St. Mary Chapel. Despite its name the almshouse was always referred to by Croydonians as 'The Great Almshouse', conveying appreciation for Elias Davy's gift.

The original residents consisted of six men - Piers Stanlock the Tutor, Henry Corde, John Christmasse, John Cooke, John Tapcliff, and John Shirburne; the one woman was Elyn Umfrey. The original overseers (Master and Wardens of the Mercers' Company) were Richard Riche, John Cotford, John Reynkyn and John Baron. The Vicar of Croydon at that time was probably John Langton – he succeeded William Oliver and was in post until his death in 1467.

He was followed by William Shaldoo who, for some inexplicable reason, brought an action in chancery against John Martin, son of Elias Davy's executor. He complained that there were only three residents and no tutor in the almshouse as the others had not been replaced when they died. As the Ordinances were quite clear whose responsibility this was, the action raises questions regarding efficient management!

If the almshouse residency was in question the increase of its goods was not. By 1460 the holdings in various parts of the parish had increased by a total of eight acres: this was maintained for the rest of the 15th century but by 1516 the total was 14 acres three roods; and by 1543 (in an incomplete record) nearly 23 acres. These were scattered throughout Bensham, Waddon, Addiscombe, Croham, Scarbrook Meadows and Old Town.

The records of lands paying quit rents to the Archbishop also show parcels of land belonging to Eton College which was founded in 1441.

It is sad that the official name of the almshouse and its founder has become 'Elis David' due to an early mistranscription.

On 24 January 1451 Henry VI paid a short visit to Croydon. This must have been quite a spectacle for the residents of the almshouse as his retinue would have passed close by. They were in a good position to observe the arrivals and departures of important people to the Archbishop's manor house.

A remarkable and much respected man called Rowland Phillips became Vicar of Croydon in 1497. He was a Doctor of Divinity, a Canon of St. Paul's Cathedral and friend of Cardinal Wolsey (which brought him much trouble in later years), and known for his brilliant and sometimes controversial preaching. One of his well-known sermons was on the evils of the latest invention - printing. He was much in demand for funeral orations and was often requested by Henry VIII to preach during Lent before the Court at Greenwich. By this time there must have been a considerable number of clergy officiating at the parish church along with two chantry priests and various special chaplains. Rowland Phillips was in the post for 40 years and his downfall came with the Reformation. After eight years of misery, court appearances, a period of imprisonment and continued contentious sermons he was eventually forced to resign in 1538 for not removing the Pope's name from the parish church service books. He died a few months later.

This was a time of some confusion and anxiety, although the ordinary folk of Croydon, however concerned about their parish priest, would have gone about their everyday life in the same way as always. From 1532 churches were plundered and monasteries dissolved, including many almshouses, as most had priest wardens. The Elis David Almshouse survived because the tutor was not a priest. Bermondsey Abbey was dissolved in 1538 and initially taken over by the Crown. It later passed to the Walsingham family.

Between 1536 and 1546 many of the Archbishops' estates and

manors were granted away so that there were changes in Lordship that Croydon was fortunate to avoid. Henry VIII did purchase the Archbishop's park and 70 acres of woodland in 1540 with further lands in 1545. He was not, however, fond of Croydon, complaining that because of the damp, low-lying land, it always made him 'rheumatik'.[9]

[9] *Croydon Homes of the Past.* Paget.

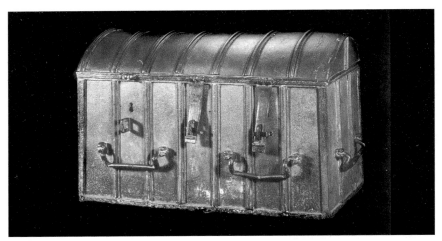

8. Common chest. 15th century.

9. The original wing of the Elis David Almshouse, Church Street. The
Victorian exterior disguises its antiquity.

10. Henry VI by unknown artist.

CHAPTER FOUR: THE 16th CENTURY

The effects of the Reformation and Dissolution and the ensuing religious uncertainty took up much of the 16th century. The elderly and sick were without many of their established support systems; 800 hospitals in England were greatly reduced in number and it was as a consequence of this that parishes made whatever provision they could to cope with the needs of their parishioners. Many almshouses were founded at this time.

It would seem likely that the Little Almshouse was founded in the late 1530s and certainly supported by the parish of Croydon (no record can be found of any endowment or personal founder). It was situated on that part of the land called Delles north of the river Wandle where, in 1447, there was one cottage amidst farmland. Today we know this site as the Reeves Corner island. It was in place by 1539 when Henry Wood of Waddon, yeoman, bequeathed the nine residents three shillings and four pence every year at Christmas for three years[10]. He left the same to the residents of the Elis David Almshouse. His will contains the earliest known reference to the Little Almshouse.

The two almshouses were neighbours for centuries before housing development intervened. They were, however, very different, for the Elis David Almshouse was financially secure and admission to it carried some status (people of good character who deserved a place by nature of their contribution to the community). The Little Almshouse was always

---

[10] Will of Henry Wood of Waddon. TNA PROB11/28 25-26.

the poor relation, struggling to survive and dependent on the goodwill of the parishioners and many small charitable legacies. Provision was made for care of the sick in the Elis David Almshouse; the Little Almshouse residents got by as best they could – sometimes whole families moved into the tiny rooms to assist their elderly relatives.

The Little Almshouse corner was an important area, being the junction with Church Road and the route to London and also the site of the Hand Cross.

By 1548 the population of Croydon was estimated to be about 1,600 souls, poverty and the problems of older age increasing proportionately. In 1545, John Hatcher, who held the manor of Norbury, bequeathed two loads of bavins (wood) to the poor of the parish each year at Christmas. This was two years before the chantry of St. Nicholas was dissolved.

In 1556 Mary Tudor spent a whole month (19 August – 17 September) at the Archbishop's manor house. According to the memoirs of her lady-in-waiting, Ann Dormer, she would sometimes dress plainly and visit the poor in their cottages accompanied only by an attendant. As the two almshouses were only a short distance from the main gate it could be speculated that her perambulations might have included their residents.

In 1559 Richard Hastinges, wax chandler of London and Faversham, Kent, left the remainder of his estate, after personal bequests, to the poor in the almshouse at Croydon called 'the lyttle almes howse'. 10 years later, William Tyrell of Croydon, who had a built a 'house of office' (a pantry or a privy) at the Elis David Almshouse, waived the overdue payment for this work in return for releasing his executors from the rent of a meadow.

In 1566 (sealed 6 August) Archbishop Parker, in conjunction with the vicar (Richard Finch) and governors, revised the Ordinances of the Elis David Almshouse, adjusting the religious observances to make them more in keeping with the Church of England's Protestantism. In the preamble to the changes the Archbishop writes: 'And understanding by Report and Suite made unto us for the great decay of the Revenues, Charters, Estcripts and other muniments of the Almshouse...'[11] Two-and-a-half centuries later the governors would accuse these sixteenth-century residents of embezzling the property and losing the common seal and writings. The Mercers' Company was likewise accused of neglecting its duties. This contributed to the need for the revision.

One of the changes stated that the vicar should hold the second key to the chest (the other two remaining with the tutor and the eldest resident). The residents' allowances were temporarily reduced and paid quarterly until 'the Revenues of the said Almshouse may be better increased'. The tutor and eldest resident were to present full accounts to the governors annually and there was to be more control over the use of the seal. The collector of rents was to be one of the governors who would also pay the residents their allowance. There was to be closer supervision.

With its poor drainage, mud and damp, Croydon was not a healthy place for those living in the lower-lying areas. Like everywhere else close

---

[11] MCA 1/23/37 Ordinances amended by Archbishop Parker.

to the city, Croydonians were terrorised by the threat of plague - a loose term covering various infectious diseases including typhus, typhoid, bubonic and pneumonic plague. In 1582 plague was rampant in London, and the women living in the Little Almshouse were particularly forbidden to go out of the town or parish 'to keep any sick person or persons without the consent of the Vicar, Bayliffe, Constables and Churchwardens' upon payne of EVERY woman of the said almshouse to be 'bannyshed the said town' and 'to loose their dwellings' until it be 'thought good' by those above-mentioned to allow them to return.[12]

One year later Archbishop Grindall gave Samuel Finch, the Vicar of Croydon, and other trustees £50 to invest in property in Waddon for the benefit of the Little Almshouse. This was later increased by Roland Kilner, a steward of Archbishop Whitgift, who invested in property in South End for the same purpose. Among his trustees was Richard Whitgift, brother of the Archbishop. Roland Kilner also replaced Elias Davy's almshouse chest with a further - and stronger - one.

In 1596 the Hospital of the Holy Trinity, Archbishop John Whitgift's almshouse was founded, and became fully operational and opened its doors to the first residents in 1599. Locally it has always been referred to as 'The Hospital' or 'The College'. The Elis David Almshouse was relegated to second place in the Croydon Almshouse hierarchy and Elias Davy's great gift to Croydon was never seen in the same light again!

---

[12] Minute Book of Homage Jury. Vol. 1, p5.

11. Engraving of 1842. Croydon Church (north side) showing the 15th century porch through which the almshouse residents would have entered.

12. Engraving of St. John's Church, Croydon (south side). 19th century.

13. Retrospective drawing of the Great Hall of the Archbishop's Manor House (Palace).

54

CHAPTER FIVE: THE 17th CENTURY

The 17th century brought drama and violence with plague, fire, civil war and the 11 years of the Commonwealth (1649-60). These were vivid events that had their effect on Croydon. The plague was responsible for 158 deaths in 1603. The population of Croydon rose to 2,600 people by 1678. The Middle Row area had become a seething mass of tenements, shops and inns with bad drainage and narrow streets full of filth. At the beginning of the century there were 30 inns and alehouses with at least a further six unlicensed houses; by 1613 these had been reduced to seven inns and 19 alehouses - still considered to be excessive!

It was, however, a fruitful century for the Little Almshouses which received some substantial bequests to ensure its security. In 1609 Francis Tyrell, Citizen of London and grocer (who gave Croydon its first Town Hall), died in Croydon leaving both the Elis David and Little Almshouses 40 shillings each. His will specified that, if he were to die and be buried in London, his funeral was to be attended by 100 bachelors for whom he provided new gloves.

In 1617 Lady Ann Allott, widow of Sir John Allott, Citizen of London and fishmonger, who had died during his mayoral year, died leaving £3 yearly to the Little Almshouse to be administered through the Company of Fishmongers. This is still received and these days amounts to about £40. Prior to her marriage to Sir John, Lady Ann had been a widowed member of the Mellish family of Sanderstead.

Two years later Sir William Walter granted land to Croydon, including a gravel pit situated on Duppas Hill, for use on the highway. The present Elis David Almshouse is now on this site which probably accounts for the low level of half of the building.

In her will dated 1628, Joan Price (who died in 1635) left to the Little Almshouse an annual income of 20 shillings through the rent of her lands and properties. Joan was the grand-daughter of William Milles Snr, who came to Croydon from Gloucestershire and acquired property in several areas including what is now Surrey Street. He died in January 1568 and was buried in Croydon Parish Church. His eldest son and heir, William, one of Croydon's eminent Elizabethans, became clerk to the Privy Council. He amassed considerable wealth, owning property in London, Gloucestershire and Croydon. He was a very religious man and generous with his riches.

He died in July 1608 and in his lengthy will, full of biblical quotes, he left many charitable bequests and some of his properties to his niece, Joan, whose mother Margaret was his sister. Joan had married John Price, described by her uncle in his will as his 'Faithful and loving servant', and they had conscientiously followed his tradition of benefactions to the poor. One of the properties involved was a grand house with orchards and gardens; today this would be behind Murray's Meat Market and the adjacent property in Surrey Street. Joan had further land and properties at Pitlake. She is often incorrectly recorded as being the earliest benefactor of the Little Almshouse in 1528 when in fact the date should be 1628. It is thought that this error occurred when the Benefactors' Board at the back of the parish church was repainted.

In 1625 Bartholomew Bannister, gentleman, left 20 shillings to the residents of the Elis David and Little Almshouses. A prominent Croydonian at this time was Edward Arnold, brewer, who lived next door to the Milles property in Butchers Row (Surrey Street). He would sometimes store his barrels of ale in his neighbour's cellars. Edward Arnold became wealthy and was involved with a number of different aspects of parish life. He is often quoted as being a benefactor of the Little Almshouse, and this may well be the case, but no will can be found to substantiate it.

Evidence, however, is available for the generous gift in 1625 of £1000 for the poor of Croydon from Henry Smith, Citizen and salter of London, alderman and philanthropist. He was an extremely wealthy man who gave £1000 to each parish in Surrey at some time. A story often attributed to him was that he walked through every parish dressed in poor clothing accompanied by a dog, and left money to those parishes where he was not whipped as a beggar and thrown out. It is now thought more likely that the story is in fact attributed to Dog-Smith, the Lambeth Pedlar, who behaved in a similar fashion in Lambeth, where he left an acre of ground.

The London records of Henry Smith were burned in the Great Fire so that very little is known about him. He lived in Silver Street, Cheapside, and was an alderman for Farringdon Without. He died a widower with no children on 30 January 1627/8 and was buried 14 February in Wandsworth Parish Church, in which parish he is believed to have been born.

The Henry Smith Charities are still in existence today, particularly in London. Croydon invested his gift in land at Deptford (in 1641) and Limpsfield (in 1630), the rents eventually used to finance the Little Almshouse.

The meadows and fields of Deptford became the New Cross Inn and the New Cross Road of today. Stockenden Farm at Limpsfield, is, however, almost exactly the same today as it was then, apart from one missing hedgerow. Still there is the beautiful old farmhouse with its many ancient features. It was originally built as a timber-framed, early Wealden Yeoman's house. Records of the occupants and owners of the farm go back to 1260.

In 1641, Adam Torlesse, faithful servant of Archbishop Laud, died and left to the 'nyne poore people of the Little Almshouse... 10 shillings a piece' to buy them some winter garments. He also left a further £5 for the poor of the parish and £10 to the parish church. This latter sum was used to purchase a silver guilt flagon which was inscribed, 'The guift of Adam Torles to Croydon Church 1641'. Among his many bequests was a sum of £100 to 'The Archbishop under whom I have lived and served above fortie years'; but the Archbishop was never to receive it for he was already in prison and would be executed in 1645, a result of his support for Charles I.[13]

Whilst the prospect was brighter for the Little Almshouse, the Elis David Almshouse was again in trouble, for in May 1627 the Mercers' Company recorded that the land of the almshouse was 'thought to be

[13] Will of Adam Torlesse. Paget Notebook 14. PCC 116 Evelyn.

diminished' with the residents receiving only £13 per annum, less than its true value.[14] The matter was to be investigated, but the outcome is unknown.

1642 saw Civil War and the Interregnum. Croydonians witnessed Thomas Fairfax and his army based at the Greyhound Inn. Sir William Brereton, a General from the Cheshire Forces, took over the Archbishop's Manor, and a parishioner called Bleeze smashed the windows of the parish church for two shillings and sixpence a day - an act that later earned him excommunication.

Order - and the monarchy - were restored in 1660. But Croydon's problems were far from over.

In 1660, a Dr William Clewer from Northamptonshire manoeuvred himself into being appointed Vicar of Croydon whilst there was no Archbishop in post to examine his credentials, and subjected the parish to his villainous ways. Aside from his penchant for gambling and thieving, his main interest lay in extorting money at every opportunity from his parishioners and subjecting them to blackmail and litigation with extraordinary success. The battleground was mainly the tithes, for these had been contentious and unpopular for some time. He made extortionate demands, lied in court, made false claims for church services and other duties where payment was involved, raising his income from £60 per year to £250 or more.

With regard to the almshouses, he demanded half of every resident's allowance and made it impossible for them to refuse. As Vicar of Croydon

---

[14] MCA 1/23/26 Copy of an extract from the minutes of the Acts of Court.

he was trustee to a great many charities and was able to abuse trust to his very good advantage. He even helped himself to the poor box saying that there was none poorer than he!

The parishioners eventually rebelled and organised themselves accordingly, taking him to court several times, indeed in 1673 the whole year was taken up with litigation and appeals. He seemed to thrive on this and totally disregarded any decisions against him! Eventually he was forced to resign in 1684 for neglect of his clerical duties, but Croydon had been severely damaged during his 24 years. Almsgiving and charitable trusts were greatly reduced, the gentry left the town, the school suffered with reduced intakes and Croydon became a place to avoid.

He moved to London where he died in March 1702 aged 75 and was buried at St. Bride's Fleet Street, near Fleet prison.

Vicars of Croydon have generally been distinguished, talented and caring priests who have often moved on to higher office; the number of those found wanting has been fortunately very small.

Charitable bequests to the Little Almshouse during these troubled times were sustained by George Mellish, a relative by marriage of Lady Ann Allott, who left £3 in 1653. Arnold Goldwell, of an old and wealthy Croydon family, left £40 in 1655 'to build upper chambers with chimneys in them to the Little Almshouse on the north side of the stone bridge near the church'.[15] In 1674, Robert Judery, blacksmith of Waddon, bequeathed three shillings and four pence.

[15] Will of Arnold Goldwell. TNA PROB11/246 213-214.

14. Croydon's first Town Hall: gift of Francis Tyrell, a benefactor of both Elis David and Little Almshouses, who died in 1609.

The Monument of Henry Smith Esq.
in the Church of Wandsworth Surry

Printed by C. Hullmandel.

15. Monument of Henry Smith in Wandsworth Parish Church, who died 30 January 1627.

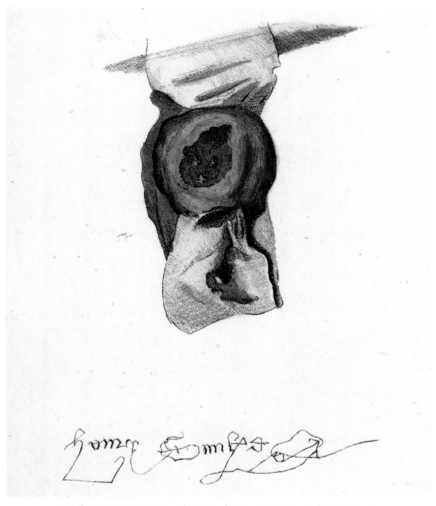

16. Seal and signature of Henry Smith reproduced from his will.

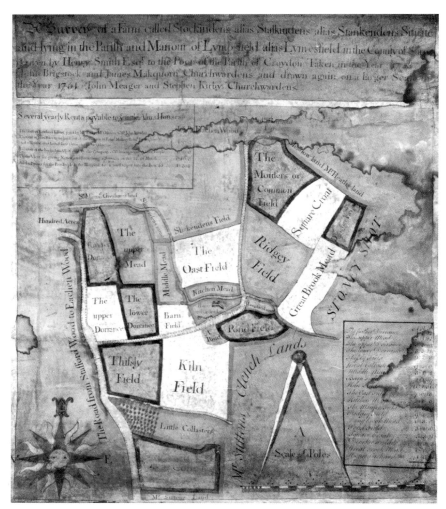

17. Enlarged plan (1751) of Stockenden Farm of 1722. Croydon Charity of Smith's Stockenden.

18. 1999 view of what were the fields and orchards of the Croydon Charity of Smith's Deptford. Sold by the trustees in 1980.

C1. The Map Tapestry, by Philip Sanderson and Caron Penney. The Tapestry Studio, West Dean, wool weft, gold thread & wool warp, 1998, based on a detail from a map of London dated 1547-1559, showing the first Mercers' hall (built 1517-24) before its destruction in the great Fire of 1666.

C2. Mercers' Company Maiden by Sir Henry St George, Richmond Herald, from the *Book of Wardens' Arms*, pen and ink on vellum, 1634.

C3. Stockenden: the original farmhouse of Henry Smith's Croydon Charity, sold by the trustees in 1918.

C4. Residents and Staff of the Elis David Almshouse, Duppas Hill Terrace, in 2004. The author is at left-hand side of back row. *Photo: Geremy Butler.*

CHAPTER SIX: THE 18th CENTURY

Increased awareness of the state of charities was an important feature of the 18th century. The population of Croydon, still on the increase, reached 4,750 by the middle of the century. Croydon continued to be a centre for travellers with its many inns and provision for stables and change of horses, boosting the town's economy. This was also a century of violent storms - disastrous when so much depended on successful harvesting of crops. In 1728 there was a devastating thunderstorm with hailstones 8-10 inches round; cattle were found drowned in the ditches and properties damaged. This was repeated in 1744 and again in 1787 when the corn crop was ruined and Old Town flooded.

Another event of concern to the parish was a fire in the roof of the middle chancel of the church on 11 March 1735, supposedly caused by negligent plumbers. Fortunately, it was discovered and extinguished within a couple of hours, but in that time £50 worth of damage had been done.

The management of the various parish charities had been, up to then, haphazard. Some had trustees originally named by the donor and passed on through families. Others were invested in the vicar and churchwardens, sometimes with the addition of various householders or persons of good repute within the parish. Much depended on knowledge being passed by word of mouth, for deeds had been lost, often in fires or by human error. The need for an efficient system of administration was recognised.

At the back of the parish church were three Benefactor Boards, the contents of which were recorded in 1721. The information on them was not altogether accurate, as can be seen with regard to Joan Price when a repainting of her date altered by 100 years.[16]

The details on the boards are too long to mention fully here but included under the heading 'under the direction and management of the churchwardens and vestry' were:

- The gift of Henry Smith mentioning 'the farm of Stackinden [sic] in Lympsfield, Surrey ...now lett for £50 per ann.', and the 'farm and lands at Deptford in Kent, now lett for £49 10sh. per ann.'
- The gift of Archbishop Edmund Grindall of £50 to invest for the benefit of the Little Almshouse.
- The seven acres of land near the Hermitage (acquired from Edward Croft in 1614 for the poor of the parish).
- A gravel pit near Dubbers Hill given to the parish by Sir William Walter of Wimbledon.
- 'The Little Almshouse, being nine small low inconvenient houses, wherein are usually placed the parish poor.'

Under the heading, 'Such as have been incorporated with governors and visitors appointed by the founders, or vested in trustees who have the power and direction thereof' were:

---

[16] LPL MS 1129.

- The Great Almshouse founded by Ellis Davy, Citizen and Mercer of London, in the year 1443 *[sic]*.
- The Hospital of the Holy Trinity founded by Archbishop John Whitgift.

Other charities were mentioned concerning education and the poor of the parish.

It is likely that, by now, the Little Almshouse was less a place for the elderly and provided a shelter for people of all ages within its tiny rooms.

At a vestry meeting of 1726 there was discussion on the rising number of the poor within the parish. It was decided to build a parish workhouse on Duppas Hill using the site of Sir William Walter's gravel pit. An Act of Parliament in 1722 (Knatchbull's Act) encouraged the setting-up of workhouses, and in such a way that their harsh regimes and strict rules would force the unfortunate inmates to obtain employment elsewhere as soon as possible.

The Croydon Workhouse on Duppas Hill was open and functioning by the end of 1727, financed by the collection of the 'Poor Rate' (fixed half yearly by the vestry) from the occupiers of all houses, tenements and lands by the overseers (elected by the vestry). The poor rate was very unpopular and it was not unusual for there to be great difficulty in extracting the payments from disgruntled parishioners.

The workhouse inmates were put to work for long hours and their meagre wages were taken for their upkeep; once in the clutches of the establishment it was difficult to find the wherewithal to extract oneself.

Some people were given allowances or a payment towards basic necessities (such as shoes) but remained in their own homes. The residents of the Little Almshouse sometimes fell into this category, often claiming parish relief because they could not afford to pay for medicines or care when they were sick.

During the 18th century, Croydonians with infectious diseases (primarily smallpox) were sent to the Pest House in Lambert Place. The women of the workhouse were sent to nurse them – an unpopular task.

With the founding of the workhouse, the Little Almshouse gained a small amount of status. Greater effort was made to concentrate on the elderly although there seemed to be no further provision for their care when frail or sick.

An incomplete survey of Elis David lands and property compiled in 1751 shows land and property at Croham, several properties and land near the Fish Market, properties near the Greyhound (an important coaching inn), properties and gardens in Scarbrook Lane, gardens and orchards in Church Street, land near Pitlake, property and land next to the George, and properties near the church.

The Archbishop's Visitation Report of 1758, submitted and signed by the Vicar, John Vade, describes the parish as 30 miles in circumference, fairly circular, being possibly four or five miles in diameter with about 1000 houses, with hamlets called Waddon, Shirley and Addiscombe.

The report also states that 'families of note [were] chiefly those of London Merchants and traders.'

John Vade was also Vicar of Rochester and his ignorance of Croydon came, perhaps, from spending such little time there, although he declared Croydon his principal residence. There is no mention of the Little Almshouse and he does mention the 'David Ellis' [sic] Almshouse for seven poor people whose estate is about £40 per ann. John Vade died in 1765 and was replaced by East Apthorpe, an American from Boston, Massachusetts.

At a vestry meeting held on 24 June 1758 a committee was appointed to investigate and report on the parish charities, giving their opinion as to underletting and other diversities.

In 1759 Joseph Williams, in a very long and detailed will, left £100 in trust for bread for the poor of the parish (excluding those in the workhouse) to be given on Christmas and New Year's Day. Trustees were appointed by the vestry to administer this very welcome legacy.

In 1760 the Tables of Benefaction in the church were updated and more financial detail added although some errors were, of course, perpetuated. These boards became the focus of attention and some of the later enquiries were based upon their information. There were several subsequent meetings regarding the Hermitage Lands, the trustees and accounts for which having become muddled. Eventually, new trustees were appointed and measures made for the income from the estate to provide the now 12 poor people of the Little Almshouse with 40 shillings quarterly to be equally divided among them.

During the examination of the state of the charities it became apparent that Stockenden Farm and the lands at Deptford, the investments of the Henry Smith Charity, were being neglected. These always suffered from being at a distance from Croydon and therefore at times were forgotten. A new set of trustees were appointed on 6 June 1769 who subsequently discovered that they had a great deal to do to rectify the problems. By March 1773 John Jarrett, the tenant of Stockenden Farm was found to have 'committed a great waste'; he was threatened with prosecution but appears not to have been removed until 1783.[17]

A Bill headed 'To be Let' describes the farm as follows: 'A Messuage, Farm and Lands, called Stockendens Farm, in the Parish of Limpsfield in the County of Surrey, now in the Occupation of John Jarratt; Consisting of a Dwelling-House with Barns, Stables, and other convenient Out-Buildings, Eighty-one Acres of Arable Land, and Seventeen Acres of rich Meadow and Pasture Land, which may be easily overflowed with good Water from a rivulet which runs through the Farm, and the Premises entitle the Tenant to a Right of Commonage upon several large and fertile Commons'. Interested persons were invited to attend the Greyhound Inn on Tuesday 5 August 1783 at 10am with their proposals in writing.

The successful applicant was Martin Tamplin who occupied the farm profitably for many years.

A very significant event for Croydon was the death of Archbishop Hutton in 1758, for he was the last Archbishop to occupy the Manor House (known as the Palace since 1596). His successors deemed the

---

[17] Vestry Minutes 4 March 1773

property too old and inconvenient for use and it was eventually put up for sale in 1780.

In February 1775 The Honourable Augustus Hervey, Vice Admiral of the Blue and Rear Admiral of the White and of the Red, and shortly to become the third Earl of Bristol (18 March 1775), negotiated a 'land deal' with the Croydon parish vestry. He wished to purchase a small piece of waste land to enhance the grounds belonging to his mistress, Mary Nesbitt, at Norwood. This today adjoins Central Hill and is the site of the Convent of the Faithful Virgin and Virgo Fidelis School. Negotiations resulted in the Earl providing £150 for an extension of the Little Almshouse.

Augustus Hervey was a colourful and interesting character. His career in the navy was well documented, and his exploits with both ships and women, as recorded in his diaries and papers, provide fascinating insight into 18th-century life. He married Elizabeth Chudleigh when he was 20 and she four years older. They had a few happy days together but from then on never lived openly as man and wife, remaining legally married until his death in 1779. Elizabeth bigamously married the Duke of Kingston in 1769 which led to a case tried by the House of Lords: she was convicted but continued as the Duchess of Kingston until 1788, when she died in Paris.

Augustus Hervey was a notorious womaniser but spent the last decade of his life, apparently happily, with Mary Nesbitt, a lady as colourful as himself. Beautiful, witty and intelligent, she had been a courtesan whose clientele included the Prime Minister's secretary and other eminent men of the day. She married Alexander Nesbitt, an Irish merchant banker, who died insane and left her a wealthy widow. It was he, not Augustus Hervey as was sometimes supposed, who purchased the house and grounds at Norwood for her, an estate often visited by the rich and famous - including the King. After Augustus Hervey's death Mary Nesbitt travelled a great deal. It has been suggested that she became a British agent offering Royalist support against the revolutionary government in France, where she died in 1825 at the age of 90.

Augustus Hervey died at 3am on 22 December 1779 of 'Gout of the Stomach' (his biographer, Michael Holmes, suggests this might have been kidney failure) in a family home at St. James' Square, London. Mary Nesbitt was present. He was succeeded by his eccentric brother Frederick, Bishop of Derry, with whom he had a long-standing enmity and who unsuccessfully contested the will in which Augustus had left much to Mary Nesbitt.

The Little Almshouse extension, warmly welcomed, was to provide accommodation for a further 12 elderly inmates, bringing the total to 24. The new wing was added to the existing almshouse in Church Street at an angle of 90 degrees on what was described as 'waste ground' (Elias Davy's farm land).

The buildings were of brick with chimneys. The same height as the existing buildings for they were to join up with two doorways. The window frames, doors and some partitions were of oak and the beams and other woodwork 'good round yellow fir'. The rooms inside were whitewashed and there was a 'closit' (with shelves) beside the chimney.[18]

[18] Vestry Minutes. 22 June 1775

At least 18 people applied for the twelve rooms and those successfully elected at a meeting attended by the existing residents were:

'Sarah Shirlock Widow, Richard Withall Senior, Ann Hawkins Widow, Ann Bailey Widow, John Arrows Widow, Sarah Strong Widow, Nicholas King, John Izzard, Thomas Grover's Wife, Lucy Brown Widow, Ann Sampson Widow, and Elizabeth Oliver.'[19]

Any who were in receipt of a pension were to relinquish it. Neither were these new residents to receive the allowances granted to the original residents, which must have resulted in tension at times.

The Elis David Almshouse was undergoing its own rebuilding programme in 1782 when repair work was carried out on its ancient fabric. In preparation for this the almshouse chest with its precious contents was moved into the church for safe-keeping. Sadly, all the contents were then stolen and, at the same time, the boundary stones of the almshouse gathered up at night and deposited in a heap on its lawn; the culprits were never found in either case.

The Vicar of Croydon, East Apthorpe, suddenly and mysteriously left Croydon for London in 1793, leaving his wife to attend to his affairs before following him. He then retired to Cambridge where he died in 1816; he was succeeded by John Ireland whose ministry was not exactly trouble-free.

[19] Ibid. 5 March 1776

In 1796 the tutor of the Elis David Almshouse, Steward Farley, died and in accordance with the ordinances left his estate to the almshouse. This was never received and was much quoted in the following century when the vicar and churchwardens were accused of abuse of charity monies. Steward Farley was from a once-wealthy and distinguished Croydon family and, ironically perhaps, was one of the overseers of the poor from 1754.

More profitable, however, was the bequest of Thomas Fewson Eagles in 1798. In an elaborate will he left £200 for the poor with the proviso that the grave of his parents should be cared for. He also requested various commemorations to himself throughout the church.

The century ended with a survey of the houses belonging to the Elis David Almshouse taken from the Land Tax Book for 1799:

A tenement in Church Street occupied by	Wm Henbrey	Rent per ann. £8.
A ditto adjoining	Wm Gillingham	4.
A ditto at the back of above	Wm French	4.
A ditto adjoining	John Lister	4.
A ditto north of the almshouse	Wm Bodkin	21.
A ditto (late the Gun Public House)	Richard Messenger	24.
A barn (sold to the Railway Company)	Wm Bodkin	2.
A tenement sold to ditto	Richard Tidy	4.
A tenement at Pitlake occupied by	Abraham Chandler	3.
A garden at ditto	Abraham Chandler	6.

A tenement at ditto	Widow Hutton	3.
A ditto at Pitlake	Mathews	3.
A ditto at Pitlake	Bleeze	3.
A ditto in High Street (said to belong)	Wm Feldwick	10.
A ditto in Middle Row	John Green	10.
A ditto near the Eleven Milestone	Widow West	2.
	Total	£111.

LANDS BELONGING:

About 65 acres of arable land at Purley Farm		£130.
(supposed to be worth 40 shillings an acre per ann.)		
	Total	**£241.**

About 3 acres of Woodland in Croham Hurst

There are other Houses and Land in the possession of Messrs. W. Chatfield, W. Budgen, F. Meager, T. Brown etc.

(The allotments under the Inclosure of Waste Lands not generally known.)

The seven poor people receive each 12sh. per month Per. ann.	£54.	12sh.
Two bushel coals each (at 2sh. per bush.) 4d. per month	18.	4.
One pound tea 8shlb. Coffee 3sh. 31b Sugar 2/6-4lb.		
Soap 4sh. & 61b. Candles 6sh.each person	8.	4. 6d
A dinner at Christmas	4.	
A 1/4 hund. bavins each (yearly) from Croham Hurst	£85.	6d.
A Great Coat about every 3 years.		

19. Augustus Hervey in 1763 by Sir Joshua Reynolds.

20. Mary Nesbitt by Sir Joshua Reynolds.

21. Photograph taken in 1870 from the tower of Croydon Parish Church. The Little Almshouse is centre and the north wing of the Elis David Almshouse can be seen in the left foreground.

CHAPTER SEVEN: THE 19th CENTURY

Great changes, both national and local, took place during the 19th century. This included the development of the railways from 1803, the Croydon Canal in 1809, and various other technological developments - even the invention of the bicycle which gave people the means of independent travel but emptied the church pews on Sundays! The population of Croydon burgeoned from 5,743 in 1801, to 20,343 in 1851, to 102,697 in 1891.

The beginning of the century saw changes brought about by the Inclosure Acts which were intended to stabilise and increase food supply and protect forests and the timber supply for the navy. The Act of 1801 was passed during a time of famine when little thought was given to possible future advances and development, especially increased population.

In 1811, rumblings of discontent were heard within the parish. They culminated in a very uncomfortable six years during which the residents of the Elis David Almshouse found themselves the centre of unwanted attention.

In February 1811 Colonel Henry Haldane, retired from a distinguished career in the army, was approached by various parishioners to request his signature on a petition asking for a vestry meeting to investigate allegations of mismanagement of parochial affairs and misuse of charity money by the vicar, John Ireland, and the churchwardens, who tried to prevent the meeting taking place. The parishioners were determined and, at a defiant gathering, Henry Haldane was elected to the Chair. Resolutions to investigate the matter were made that incensed the vicar and the situation became very hostile for all concerned. Henry Haldane received several letters from the vicar that were, in his view, 'very improper'.[20]

Croydon was rife with rumour. Central to this situation were the residents of the Elis David Almshouse who were led to believe that they were being deprived of their just dues.

On 22 May 1812, Croydon was flooded with handbills circulated by Henry Haldane who had received an anonymous letter accusing him of financial dishonesty. The accusation was a side issue and was later proved to be false. He believed the perpetrator to be the vestry clerk's clerk, Thomas Read. This lead to two court cases during the following years when Thomas Read was found 'Not Guilty' and subsequently accused Henry Haldane of Perjury. Haldane was also found 'Not Guilty'. He did, however, have some powerful friends. During his career he had been aide-de-camp to Lord Cornwallis and in April 1814, seven eminent men spoke on behalf of his 'good character' in court. They included General Ross, (military secretary and Adjutant General), George Moncrombie Robinson Esq, M.P., (Director of the East India Company), and David Vanderheyden Esq, M.P. It was said in court that Lord Cornwallis himself, now dead, held Henry Haldane in the highest regard. Haldane was accustomed to authority and automatic respect. He was autocratic and forthright in his manner, but ageing. There appears to have been a

[20] MCA 1/23/18. Letter from Henry Haldane to Master and Wardens.

personality clash between him and the academic, rather arrogant and articulate Dr. Ireland.

On 25 February 1812 the Mercers' Company received a letter from a Mr Guy, a self-appointed attorney claiming to be acting on behalf of the Elis David residents, who accused the governors of deviating from the Ordinances.

On 26 October of the same year the tutor of the almshouse, James Bulley, took a petition from the residents to Mercers' Hall but was turned away.

He returned four days later with an accompanying letter from Henry Haldane and the petition was received. (It later transpired that this petition was actually penned by Henry Haldane himself and signed by the residents - some with their mark X - following a meeting in the almshouse that Haldane had chaired.) Various accusations against the governors were made that included the misappropriation of property, deviation from the Ordinances to the detriment of the almshouse, and that the charity had not been registered according to the Act of Parliament passed on 12 July that year for the securing of charitable donations.

There followed an exchange of correspondence which left the Mercers' Company in no doubt of Henry Haldane's view of the whole affair and enclosing an account of the estates as far as he could ascertain. Nothing was heard for a further month, so the residents sent another letter to the Mercers' Company:

Praying your benevolence in our affairs as our humane and charitable founder directed us to do in cases of need... we hope and trust that time has not obliterated from the breasts of the Citizens of London that benevolence and charity which existed 365 years ago in the breast of Mr Elis Davy then Citizen and Mercer of that great and opulent City.

The tutor went on to complain that they had been refused their usual winter coal allowance adding:

the evils which must result to the aged and decrepit if left without fuel during the winter months is too obvious to be mentioned. [21]

The Mercers responded with a letter to Henry Haldane requesting further details which were duly provided. In the meanwhile, the governors bestirred themselves and, with assurances to the Mercers' Company that they wanted to help, sent their 'most ready concurrence' to provide any information.[22]

It became clear that over the years procedures had lapsed and communication broken down. Both governors and overseers had deviated from the requirements and both had difficulty in locating the revised Ordinances. Mr Guy was in possession of the book published by Dr. Ducarel in 1783 on the history of Croydon in which he included the original Ordinances of the Elis David Almshouse, and his accusations

---

[21] MCA 1/23/7. Reminder of Petition from almshouse people to the Master and Wardens.
[22] Ibid.

were based on these. The residents - poor, ill-educated and aged - were ignorant of relevant matters and had little communication with the governors who held their meetings in the Kings Arms public house.

On 4 December the Mercers' representatives came to Croydon to interview the residents and governors; Henry Haldane was present at their request. The tutor was so nervous that he was quite unable to give any account of himself, let alone more complicated matters. Further meetings were planned and the Mercers' Company instigated their own inquiry. The outcome of this, together with some very long and detailed letters from Henry Haldane, revealed a complete breakdown of communication between governors and residents and ignorance of the statutory requirements. For example, no-one knew of the whereabouts of the almshouse chest and common seal (Dr Ireland blamed the residents). Yet it had been moved into the church for safe-keeping in 1782 when the contents were stolen. The current deeds and documents, such as they were, resided with the vestry clerk's clerk. The almshouse estates were a puzzle; no-one knew where the houses in the High Street had come from - or if there were two or four. A tutor, Steward Farley, had died in 1796 leaving his goods to the almshouse but the legacy appeared to be missing. The governors declared it was accounted for; in fact the documents were never passed to the almshouse but left in the care of Farley's executor who became a bankrupt, so the legacy (£56) was lost. So it went on, with discrepancies and misunderstandings. What was clear, however, was the inefficiency of the lettings procedure which was certainly not to the good of the almshouse.

The Mercers withdrew to consider the matter. Mr Guy challenged the legality of their tribunal. The vestry clerk suddenly 'remembered' certain illuminating facts and Dr. Ireland attacked the residents' mental abilities (it was said he threatened the petition's signatories with the workhouse). It was agreed that the residents should receive their allowances complete and not half in coal. Dr Ireland was invited to Mercers' Hall and, at the beginning of 1813, the governors were examined by the Mercers' Company. The Mercers pursued their own case and the eventual result was an agreement that there had been faults and misunderstandings all round. Certain changes needed to be made with regard to the lettings procedure (which took a further year for the governors to effect) and the Mercers' Company was reassured that they had carried out their statutory role as far as they were able.

It was not until 1815 that the governors at last found the amended Ordinances of 1566 which, to quote their clerk Thomas Penfold, 'Everyone has since missed'.[23]

The parishioners then turned their attention to the other charities under the trusteeship of the church and vestry officials and brought action in chancery in 1815 and 1816, accusing them of mismanagement of both Smiths Charities and the Hermitage Estates.

Henry Haldane had become a great champion for the residents and his tenacity in getting to the root of the problems resulted in a new era of cooperation between the governors and the Mercers' Company, and a better awareness of the past. The state of the charity had been

---

[23] MCA 1/23/24. Letter from Thomas Penfold to Mr. Edward Ward.

brought to the attention of everyone concerned, and, eventually, led to more formalised and controlled administration, ending up with the Charity Commissioners later in the century. Dr. Ireland left Croydon in 1816 to become Dean of Westminster and Henry Haldane moved from Croydon.

In 1815 the artist John Singleton Copely died and his body was interred in the north wall of Croydon Parish Church. During the digging of his grave the bones of Elias Davy were disturbed - an accident which greatly upset the people of Croydon and which received coverage in the newspapers of the day.

In June 1819, in accordance with an Act of Parliament of the same year, a Select Vestry was elected, 'For the care and management of the Concerns of the Poor of this Parish'.

This committee presented a report to a meeting of the vestry, on 31 January 1821, detailing its investigation into the estates and charities belonging to the parish. It revealed the ignorance of the charities involved, their origins and directives, neglected rent collection and lack of proper accounting.

The result was the application to the courts for a Scheme for Application of Rents arising from Parish Charities, monthly meetings with church wardens and overseers, and a proper method of accounting recorded in a book open to public scrutiny. Those who would benefit from the charities were to be 'Not given to excessive drinking or immoral lives' who had resided at least five years in Croydon. This, of course, would apply to the residents of the Little Almshouse, while the Elis David residents operated within their own ordinances.

From then on the 'State of the Charities' received regular attention, although a number of errors were perpetuated. In 1825, a report was published by the 'Commission to Inquire concerning the Charities in England and Wales.' The unsatisfactory management of charities led to the setting-up of the Charity Commission with the Charitable Trusts Act of 1853.

Obliged to report on such matters, the Select Vestry of 11 February 1830 noted that:

> The Little Almshouses were in a bad state of repair and that the funds from which the same were accustomed to be defrayed, were so reduced that they were no longer of a sufficiency to be defrayed out of them.

Necessary repairs were to be carried out and financed from the Poor Rate. Much less money was given voluntarily to support the ever-increasing number of poor. Significant for Croydon were the institution of daughter churches within the parish from 1829. These had their own parochial districts whose parishioners were, understandably, reluctant to continue financing the poor of the larger parish.

The 1841 census for the Little Almshouse shows that there was a total of 37 people in the small rooms provided for 24, aged between 90 and seven. There was, of course, no warden and the younger persons were probably family members there to assist their aged relative. Six of the residents were male. The eight Elis David residents ranged from 90 to 70 years of age and the 90-year-old had a 45-year-old with her; four of the residents were male.

In 1846, the governors requested the Mercers' Company to investigate problems at the Elis David Almshouse. Edward Page, the tutor, and resident John Hobbs were found guilty of disorderly and improper conduct. The tutor was suspended from office and both men had their allowances halved. The Master and Wardens of the Mercers' Company donated their travelling expenses of 13 shillings and four pence, together with the £1. 6sh. 8d. paid to them in accordance with the Ordinances, to be distributed amongst the residents, excluding Edward Page and John Hobbs.

In 1847 the Mercers' Company consented to the granting of building leases for the charity: no further details are available on this matter.

The 1851 census return for the Little Almshouse shows 24 *bona fide* residents aged between 60 to 90 of which seven were male. There were three married couples. Only four residents were actually born in Croydon, and there were nine extra people: five grand-daughters, one daughter and three visitors. The entry for the Elis David Almshouse shows eight residents aged between 89 and 64, plus a 49-year-old widow with a 65-year-old resident.

In his will proved 6 May 1852, John Blake, auctioneer, left £1000 to be invested for 'Benefit of the Inmates of the Little Almshouse'. John Blake came from a wealthy family and held several properties in the parish including the one adjacent to the workhouse in Duppas Hill Terrace.

There were several substantial bequests during the latter half of the 19th century which included £50 from Thomas Field for the Little Almshouse in 1857, £1000 in a trust fund from John Budgen, clock and watchmaker in 1869, £5,106 from his friend William Inkpen, coach proprietor, in part to be used for the benefit of the 'Inmates of the Little Almshouses' as an allowance and for coal in 1873. £50 from John William Ebbutt, upholsterer and cabinet maker, was to be invested for the Little Almshouse in 1875. There were other substantial bequests to the poor of the parish, such as £1,300 from John Henry Smith in 1886, £400 from Mary Spering in 1884 to be invested for ten poor widows over 60 years of age - which may well have been used for the residents of the Little Almshouse, according to the discretion of the vicar and church wardens.

1855 brought the publication of Croydon's first local newspaper, the *Croydon Chronicle.* This was followed in 1863 by the *Croydon Observer* and in 1869 by the *Croydon Advertiser.*

These publications gave coverage to Croydon's charities: admissions to the Elis David Almshouse were congratulated on their placement; Christmas dinners (roast beef, plum pudding and strong ale) for the residents of the Little Almshouse - held in the Industrial School - were reported in full. Not so welcome were the reports in February 1881 of a fire in the Elis David Almshouse, started by an elderly resident called Mrs Dewdney, who was airing linen in front of her fire - with disastrous results.

There was always a great fear of fire for obvious reasons, and Croydonians were deeply upset by the fire on the night of 5 January 1867 that destroyed much of their ancient parish church. The cause was a faulty flue in one of the heating stoves at the west end of the church. That it gained such a hold was mainly due to the rivalry of the two local fire brigades whose haste to be first on the scene obliterated any thought of alerting the turncock at the waterworks. It was, therefore, nearly an hour before a substantial water supply was available, by which time the roof materials of dry wood, varnish and turpentine ensured an unhindered spread. It was a cold night with a covering of snow:

> The effect of the flames upon the snow clad roofs of adjacent houses together with hues of the sparks which shot upwards in large bodies, presented a spectacle of dazzling splendour and reminded one of a grand pyrotechnic display, especially when the roof fell in, when the heavens were lighted up with one huge sheet of flame. [24]

The hero of the hour was Ebenezer Whittaker, the parish clerk, who hastened to the scene and busied himself with saving the parish registers, some communion plate, the ancient lectern and a few deeds and papers. Gone were the vestments of Elias Davy along with most of the church's treasures and memorials. Elias Davy's tomb survived the fire but not the rebuilding, when it was demolished for the erection of a pillar.

The site was visited by a large number of grieving parishioners

[24] *Croydon Chronicle.* 12 January 1867.

hardly able to believe the scene of devastation that confronted them. A restoration fund was immediately set up and reconstruction commenced in November 1867. As a temporary measure, the parish was loaned an iron church erected in Scarbrook Road. This was used until the rededication on the anniversary, 5 January 1870.

Notice !

To the Inhabitants of the Parish of Croydon.

WHEREAS on this day the 22d, of MAY 1812. an ANONYMOUS LETTER was received directed to Henry Haldane Esqr. bearing Post Marks, Ludgate Hill, 8 & 10 o'Clock, 22d, of May 1812, of which the following is

A COPY.

Before you atempt to take the beem out of your Neabors Eye remove the mote from your own.

before you accuse others of peculation and robery look at home. who countenences a mother with one foot in the grave & the other scacely out to rob the cuntry every year of a larg Sum by swearing herself to be what both both you & herself KNOW SHE IS NOT

O fy upon it you asociate of

GUY FOX.

THE FACT.

The Lady referred to in the above letter has a small pension of £10. a year, (with which Colonel Haldane has no concern whatever) it is paid from the War Office, upon what is called the *Compassionate List*, and which Pension she has received from that Office from about the year 1760. now nearly 52 years—No Oath is required with respect to any circumstances attending it, but which of course are well known at the War Office.—she only makes Oath that she had received the same Pension the preceding year, and the Rev. Dr. ROSE, one of the Magistrates of the County, has had the goodness of late years, to call upon her annually to administer the Oath, and to sign the Affidavit.

The SIZE, the WATER MARKS, and all other appearances, of the paper on which the anonymous letter is written, agree exactly with those of a sheet of paper which was received from Mr. Penfold's (the Vestry Clerk) Office, under the Signature

THOMAS READ.

Col. Haldane will be much obliged to any Person who will give him such information, as shall enable him to prosecute criminally, to conviction, the Writer of the above FALSE & MALICIOUS LIBEL.

HENRY HALDANE.

Croydon, May 22, 1812.

Harding Junior Printer, Croydon.

22. Handbill produced by Henry Haldane in May 1812, in response to receiving an anonymous letter falsely accusing him of financial dishonesty.

23. Croydon Parish Church after the fire of 5 January 1867

One parishioner, George Thornton, a gardener who lived in Duppas Hill Terrace, and who many years later became the tutor of the Elis David Almshouse, wrote a poem about the fire:

The companion of the Old Church that noble elm tree!

Beneath that old elm tree, where I have oft took shelter

When coming home from school I've run all helter skelter,

And when beneath its shade I've gazed upon its tower

And thanked Him far above for giving me such power.

The bride has seen it oft, the bridegroom seen it often,

And the mourners caught a glimpse when following the coffin;

And close by this old tree, where thousands have passed the spot,

Now in dust and ashes lie almost or quite forgot.

And close by this old tree there stood a pile

Where many I have known sit down its centre aisle,

Where many Sabbath days I've spent and many a Good Friday,

And in my time have seen three good sextons, Richard, James and William Tidy.

But on a Winter's night the snow fell fast

And keenly blew the Winter's blast,

But sad to state a fire did rage

And with that pile it did engage.

It brought it to a dreadful state

But how it happened I can't state.

Now there are both rich and poor

I know, is sorry for its overthrow.

Its fine old bells I did admire

When sitting by a Winter's fire.

Now, the music of those bells are gone

And Croydon parish seems quite forlorn.

Oh! That dreadful fire! It did consume

Those splendid tablets and fine old tombs,

likewise its altar, rich and rare,

Where has been joined some happy pairs;

They have heard the organ's sweetest sounds,

But now, alas! its smouldering on the ground.

Farewell! Old Croydon Church and noble steeple;

God bless her town and all her people.

But may the old elm tree a shelter be

To many boys as it was to me.

The Vicars, I have known a few,

The first I knew I tell you true,

It was Dr. Ireland fill'd the place

And left it, but not like Dr Clewer, in disgrace.

The next that in the pulpit stood

Was the Rev. J.C. Lockwood.

The above two names are not flimsy,

But the next was the Rev. Henry Lindsay;

And to leave it was his option.

The next was the Rev. J.G. Hodgson.

When first I knew the Parish Clerk

His name, I do declare, was Jemmy Slarke;

The next succeeded in a trice,

His name was Joseph Thomas Rice;

But death came without much warning,

His son succeeded to be sworn in;

But death suddenly o'er took him in the race,

And then another took his place.

His name was Wright and Walter too,

And quite respected by all he knew.

The next, I tell you in particular,

And his name is Ebenezer Whittaker,

And, to his honour be it handed down,

He saved the registers of good old Croydon town.

The beadles I have known of old

Are dead and in the churchyard cold,

Where snow and rain and also sunbeam

Cover junior and senior poor old Pilbeam.

Now, they are dead they have run their race,

Some others now must fill the place,

Now, to choose a beadle he must be fat and hearty,

And after Pilbeam was Ned McCarthy;

But he left it before he had run his earthly race,

So after that John Julien took his place,

His time was short, it was felt most sadly;

It fell to the lot of William Bradley.

I must now conclude my simple rhymes

I've made on our Old Church, the tree and chimes,

For everything is all confusion,

I'll not attempt further allusion.

George Thornton. Croydon. January 1867.

There were many significant developments in Croydon during the latter half of the 19th century. In 1862, it was decided that a new, and larger, workhouse was required and a site at Windmill Road was obtained, opening on 25 October 1866. It remained in operation until 1923 and many Croydon residents remember that it eventually became the Queens Road (Geriatric) Hospital. The old workhouse in Duppas Hill Terrace was used as the Workhouse Infirmary until 1885 when the new Infirmary that later became Mayday (University) Hospital was opened. The Duppas Hill Terrace site was sold for residential development and the proceeds were put towards the Poor Rate.

The 1861 census cannot be relied upon as the enumerator misnamed the almshouses. The entries for 1871 show 18 residents in the Little Almshouse aged between 84 and 62 of which one was male; two of the residents were former school mistresses. There were two visitors. In the Elis David Almshouse were nine residents which included one married couple. The ages ranged from 61 to 84; there were four males. Occupations were given as nurse, monthly nurse (who attended mothers after birth), annuitant, formerly needlewoman, formerly bricklayer, and formerly farm tenant.

The 1881 census entry for the Little Almshouse records 22 residents of which one was male with ages ranging from 62 to 90. There were an extra five people presumably to look after their relative. Occupations were given as 'Inmate of Almshouse'.

In 1875 the Elis David Almshouse was enlarged for 12 and the 1881 census return therefore records 16 residents of which four were married couples. There were 6 males, the age range was 68-82 and occupations, apart from 'Inmate of Almshouse' were gardener, tailor and carpenter.

In 1891 the Little Almshouse had 24 residents aged 68 to 91 of which there were no males. There were six others of which three were children aged nine, 11 and 14 plus three to assist an elderly resident.

The Elis David Almshouse had been enlarged for 20 in 1887 so the 1891 census records 27 residents aged between 87 and 65 of which there were nine married couples and ten males. There were two vacancies. One resident of 80 had a daughter of 48 with her and it is difficult to know if she was a temporary visitor or a *bona fide* resident. The entry suggests the latter.

The Vicars of Croydon have always been of importance to the Elis David and Little Almshouses for much has depended on their interest and enthusiasm for their statutory role within the charities. A giant of a man in every sense, John Masterman Braithwaite was instituted as vicar in 1882. His keenness and energy for all aspects of his parochial duties became legendary and he was held in great esteem throughout the county. He was known as a man who 'got things done' and his achievements were many. He was an active member of the Croydon Schools Board, instituted the Parish Church Schools, was a Governor of the Whitgift Foundation, was responsible for the new Welcome Hall, was Hon. Chaplain to Croydon General Hospital, and the First V.B. the Queens Regiment. He opened and established the Croydon Church Institute and the Pitlake Mission. He was a great friend to the poor and elderly and was often to be found in the almshouses. Sadly, his ministry in Croydon was cut short when he died suddenly of heart failure on 28 June aged 43. His legacy of good works lives on even today. The Braithwaite Hall was named after him as a tribute to his work supporting a free library.

In 1887, the Elis David Almshouse was enlarged by a new wing for 12 residents. This was partly financed by a gift from Charles Overton, who also paid for railings and a gate. The rest of the money came from the almshouse charity itself. Charles Overton was the oldest surviving son of Henry whose gas works provided Croydon with its first gas lamps. Charles Overton died on 26 September 1895 and bequeathed £1000 to the Elis David Almshouse in a trust fund.

The century ended with a flourish for the town with major reconstruction taking place in the - by then - slum area between Surrey Street and what had become the High Street. The Croydon Improvement

Scheme of 1890 removed a hotchpotch of ancient and decrepit tenements, shops, inns and boarding houses, widened the High Street and replaced it with much of today's layout. There were four properties belonging to the Elis David Almshouse involved in this reorganisation.

Attention had been given to Croydon's 'State of the Charities' throughout the second half of the century with accounts published in local papers and well attended – sometimes stormy - vestry meetings. Parishioners felt that they were never given full information and in 1871 the Charity Commissioners held a Court of Inquiry that suggested putting all the charities apart from the Whitgift Foundation under one elected management committee. A proposal was made to this effect in the vestry meeting of 7 April 1874 and the following April a committee was formed to develop this. There followed several years of procrastination and confusion as various individual trustees, particularly those of the Smith's Deptford Charity, opposed the idea. Eventually a proper proposal was made that led to the schemes of 1893, amalgamating 19 separate charities in the parish of Croydon under the title 'The Croydon Charities of Henry Smith and Others'. This was approved by the Charity Commissioners on 28 April 1893. A similar separate Scheme for the Administration of the Almshouse Charity of Elis David was approved by the Charity Commissioners on 5 May 1893.

The schemes were long and detailed and need not be discussed here, but from then on the governors became trustees, still including the vicar and church wardens, with an employed clerk. The trustees were to be the same for both schemes except for the addition of a member of the Mercers' Company for the Elis David Charity. These schemes were amended and revised from time to time and administration of the various charities inevitably became regulated and more efficient.

Under the schemes of 1893 the almshouse residents (between 30 and 40 in number for the Little Almshouse and not more than 24 for Elis David) were to be poor persons of good character of either sex having lived in the parish for not less than five years. During that time they were not to have been in receipt of Poor Law relief and to be unable to support themselves by virtue of age, ill-health, accident or infirmity. The allowances for the Elis David residents were to be between 8-12 shillings a week and the Little Almshouse residents between 8-10 shillings. In both almshouses the residents were not to be absent for longer than 24 hours without permission from the trustees or clerk. Residents could be removed for insobriety, insubordination, breach of regulations, immoral or unbecoming conduct, receiving Poor Law relief, and mental disease.

The 1893 Scheme for the Elis David Charity recorded holdings of property and land as follows:

Church Street: Almshouse

House and shop (Reeves)

79, 80 and 81.

Elis David Road: 3 houses - 1 with shop.

Land

Labourers Dwellings

(N.B. all above on The Land called Delles.)

High Street:	4 (Hooker and Webb) and 6 (Coffee Tavern)
	Rent charge on house
King Street:	13 and 14.
Scarbrook Hill:	3 houses
Pitlake:	Houses, shops and land.
North End:	2 houses with shops
	Railway Bell Inn (part).
Brighton Road:	House with shop
	6 houses
	Land and cottages
Croydon Common:	House and land
Lower Addiscombe Road:	Land
South Norwood:	Land and 2 houses
Thornton Heath:	Land
Croham Dean:	Lands and garden
Sanderstead:	Lands

The Elis David Almshouse was secure and flourishing.   However, the ancient buildings of the Little Almshouse were 'dilapidated and insanitary'.[25] A site exchange took place with the Whitgift Foundation for a plot of land in Scarbrook Road where a new almshouse for 32 residents was erected. The old site in Church Street was eventually utilised by the Reeves family for a development of their business.

---

[25] Speech by Henry Seale, Chairman of Trustees. *Croydon Advertiser*. 21 November 1896.

The Little Almshouse residents were transferred to the new almshouse in Scarbrook Road which was named after Henry Smith. The buildings were charming and remembered by older Croydonians today with great affection. They had gardens and were well situated near to the public baths.

The Henry Smith Almshouse was officially opened on 21 November 1896 by Mrs (later Lady) Elizabeth Edridge in the presence of a large number of local dignitaries including her husband, the Deputy Mayor, Frederick Edridge J.P. A service was conducted by the vicar, Henry Pereira (later Bishop of Croydon).

The new almshouse also provided a laundry, a mortuary, and a board room for the trustees (no more meetings in a local hostelry!).

Lady Edridge was a true friend and benefactor for she visited regularly, read to the residents and even paid for the funerals of at least two of them, maintaining her support until her death in 1933. She was also a great benefactor to Croydon and worked tirelessly for many charitable causes. She was much loved and at her funeral in Croydon Parish Church she was referred to as 'the greatest little lady Croydon has ever known'.[26]

The people of Croydon called the Henry Smith Almshouse 'the Little Almshouse' for many years until, for them, it became 'the Scarbrook Road Almshouse'.

[26] Address by Bishop of Croydon, the Rt. Rev'd Edward Woods. *Croydon Advertiser*. 9 December 1933.

24. The Henry Smith Almshouse. View from the Flyover, 1969.
Photo: John Gent

25. The Henry Smith Almshouse facing north-west.

26. The Henry Smith Almshouse facing south-east (towards Scarbrook Road).

27. The site of the Henry Smith Almshouse in 2000.

28. Lady Elizabeth Edridge.

29. South Wing of the Elis David Almshouse, Church Street (now Ramsey Court) erected 1887. Gift of Charles Overton.

30. The railings and gate of the Elis David Almshouse, Church Street (now Ramsey Court). Originally the gift of Charles Overton.

CHAPTER EIGHT: UP TO DATE

The 20th century saw two world wars, a reconstructed Croydon, and advances in transport and communication. The population of Croydon increased to an estimated 335,600 in 1997.

The 1901 census records 13 men and 30 women residents in the Henry Smith Almshouse of which 12 were married couples with an age range of 57 to 90. Three were born in Croydon, plus a sick nurse worker of 58: one daughter and one grand daughter.

In the Elis David Almshouse were ten men and 28 women of which six were married couples. The age range was 59-79: six were born in Croydon.

This century also brought a further benefactor, Dr Evelyn Lancelot Adams, who donated money and his house in St. James' Road in memory of his father, Irishman Dr. Thomas Rutherford Adams and his first wife, Janet McKenzie Campbell, who had died in February 1922. Dr Adams went down in Croydon's history as being opposed to the National Health Service. Today, the site of his house is a garden centre.

In 1918 Stockenden Farm was sold, the trustees unappreciative of its beauty, history and uniqueness until it was too late. The present owner of the farm has been there since 1956 (in a modern bungalow), as have the owner-occupiers of the wonderful old farmhouse. Smith's Deptford was sold in 1980, the money from this sale, like many of the inherited legacies, being invested in bonds, stocks and shares. In 1962 the Elis

David residents received £1.1.8d a month, 32 hundredweight of gift coal and 167 bundles of firewood; every 19 September they each received £1 from the Overton trust fund.

By the early 1960s much discussion had been given to an enlarging of the Elis David Almshouse, possibly adding land fronting Church Road and St. John's Grove. Croydon, however, was planning great changes in road and building construction and almshouse plans were put on hold to await council decisions. Once made, further negotiations resulted in an exchange of land with the council for the site in Duppas Hill Terrace where the two almshouses could be amalgamated in a new building. This new almshouse for over 80 residents was to carry the (mistranscribed) nomenclature of the earliest and most important benefactor, Elis David (Elias Davy).

A new scheme sealed on 27 September 1974 amalgamated the charities. The 20 trustees included: the vicar and church wardens of Croydon Parish Church (ex-officio trustees), three nominative trustees which included a member of the Mercers' Company and two London Borough of Croydon councillors. The remaining trustees were co-optative.

The 54 residents of Elis David and Henry Smith Almshouses were transferred into the new building, a move that was anticipated with mixed feelings and some misunderstanding as local inhabitants protested that the elderly were being forced from their homes. Both protest and explanation were to be found in the pages of the local papers.

The two almshouses in previous schemes had supported Out Pensioners - financial assistance to people in their own homes as had been practised for centuries before formalisation in 1893. In 1974, therefore, the new title of Croydon Almshouse and Relief in Need Charities was instituted, and it is still known as such today.

The original Elis David Almshouse building in Church Street was renamed Ramsey Court and, sad to say, there is no indication to passers-by of its history or origins, or that it was one of Croydon's historic treasures. It does, however, provide offices for other charities. The site of the Little Almshouse in Church Street is now a very busy Reeves Corner island; whilst the site of the Henry Smith Almshouse in Scarbrook Road is a car park.

In May 1979 the Croydon Almshouse Charities joined the Almshouse Association - founded in 1949 to provide support and assistance regarding management matters for the trustees of almshouse charities. On 7 January 1999 the Director of the Almshouse Association, Maj. Gen. Anthony de C.L. Leask, CB CBE, visited the almshouse to talk with residents, staff and trustees.

History was made again during April of the millennium year when a party of residents, staff and trustees visited Mercers' Hall for a guided tour and tea. There is now a history room in the almshouse with a small permanent display which includes the framed indentures of the Henry Smith Almshouses, and 'Founders' Day' is celebrated annually with a tea party in April.

On the exterior walls are tablets taken from the old building and dated 1875 and 1887, whilst in the foyer is a list of charities and benefactors (with errors!), a photograph of Elias Davy's land purchase record and three sketches of the almshouses by late resident Lilian Morse.

Trustee meetings are held in the communal lounge around a table taken from the Henry Smith Almshouse boardroom, and on the wall are photographs of the three older almshouse buildings.

During 2004 an interior modernisation programme began with the aim of providing some enlarged flats, reducing the possible occupancy total to about 50 residents.

Almshouses today tend to sit on the sideline of the now more dynamic world of elderly care with its legislative framework and positive care programmes. Most are steeped in tradition and tend to follow their own mores handed down through the centuries. The Elis David Almshouse is no exception. From its meticulous preparation in the mid-fifteenth century as Croydon's Great Almshouse, together with its 'little' counterpart epitomising the struggle of everyday Croydon folk some ninety years later, these organisations have tenaciously survived through centuries of mayhem, national crises and local misunderstanding. They are essential components in the mosaic of Croydon's history and, indeed, its present.

31. Residents and staff of the Henry Smith Almshouse celebrating the coronation of George V in 1911.

32. The Elis David Almshouse, Church Street (now Ramsey Court) in 2004.

33. The Elis David Almshouse, Duppas Hill Terrace, in 2004.

34. Princess Alexandra, with Chairman of the Trustees Douglas Rawling, unveiling a plaque at the official opening of the Elis David Almshouse, Duppas Hill Terrace, on 25 March 1975.

35. Chairman of the Trustees, Noel Hepworth (L) and Mercer Trustee Christopher Clementi (R) outside the almshouse main entrance, in 2004.

36. North view of Croydon Parish Church in 2004.

BENEFACTORS OF CROYDON ALMSHOUSE CHARITIES

1447:	Elias Davy
1539:	Henry Wood
1545:	John Hatcher
1559:	Richard Hastinges
1569:	William Tyrell
1583:	Archbishop Edmund Grindal
1597:	Rowland Kilner
1609:	Francis Tyrell
1614:	Edward Croft
1617:	Lady Ann Allot
1625:	Henry Smith
	Bartholomew Bannister
1628:	Joan Price
	?Edward Arnold
1641:	Adam Torlesse
1653:	George Mellish
1655:	Arnold Goldwell
1674:	Robert Judery
1759:	Joseph Williams
1796:	Steward Farley
1831:	Mary Allen

1843:   Thomas Fewson Eagles

1852:   John Blake

1858:   Thomas Field

1869:   John Budgen

1873:   William Inkpen

1875:   John William Ebbutt

1884:   Mary Spering

1887 and 1895: Charles Overton

1896:   John Henry Smith

1932   (previous to): Lady Elizabeth Edridge

1934:   Dr. Evelyn Lancelot Adams

LIST OF ARCHIVES USED IN RESEARCH

1. Mercers' Company Archives
2. Croydon Local Studies Library and Archives.
3. Guildhall Library and Archives.
4. Corporation of London Record Office.
5. Drapers' Company Archives.
6. Merchant Taylors' Company Archives.
7. Society of Genealogists Library.
8. Family Record Centre.
9. London Metropolitan Archives.
10. Probate Registry.
11. National Register of Archives.
12. British Library.
13. Newspaper Library, Colindale.
14. The National Archives.
15. Surrey History Centre, Woking.
16. Lewisham Local Studies Library.
17. Southwark Local Studies Library.
18. Lambeth Palace Library.
19. House of Lords Record Office.
20. Suffolk Record Office, Bury St. Edmunds.
21. Whitgift Foundation Archives.
22. Papers belonging to Mrs Barbara Fitch, Stockenden.

23. Papers belonging to Messrs. Reeves, Church Street.

24. Croydon Parish Church Archives.

25. Charity Commissioners' Records and Archives.

26. The Museum of London.

27. J.B. Shakespeare Archives.

28. Croydon Crematorium and Cemetery Archives.

29. Bodleian Library, Oxford.

30. Ealing Local Studies Library.

31. Acton Local History Society.

32. National Maritime Museum, Greenwich.

33. Oriental and India Office Collections, British Library.

PRIMARY SOURCES

17th century copy of Elias Davy's purchase of land. BL. Royal 17B XLVII f133b/134 (MS).

Survey of lands in Croydon which paid quit-rents to the Archbishop 1486-1509. (Microfilm)
Bodleian Library Oxford MS Tanner 223 HenVII f178b.

Elias Davy's will.1455.
TNA 4 Stockton. Also CLRO MCFP/100 (Microfilm)
Codicil BL Royal 17bXLVII f96b (MS).

Ordinances of the Elis David Almshouse, 1447.
LPL Register of John Morton 1486-1500 Vol I f199-202 (Microfilm).

TNA. C1 6/69 (MS).
> Bundle 6 page 27 suit 69 Vol. 1 Chancery Proceedings Seizure of goods. Thomas Fauconer.

GL   The History of Parliament:

The House of Commons 1386-1421

Members E-O p59-62 Thomas Fauconer.

LPL Reg. Henry Chicele

Vol.4 pp88-92 Latin English p 90 Canterbury and York Society Cathine Fauconer.

Selden Society. Records of Statutory Recognizances

English Translation of Burton v Davy

Publications of The Selden Society. Vol. 49, 1932 pp117-119

TNA Early Chancery Proceedings 28/417-418

William Oliver 1440.

GL   (Ed.) A.H. Thomas, *Calendar of Plea and Memoranda Rolls of the City of London*. 1413-1437, Cambridge University Press,1943.

(Ed.) Reginald R. Sharpe, *Calendar of Letter Books of the City of London,1350-1497,* 11 Vols. 1899-1912.

Rev. Alfred Beaven, *The Aldermen of the City of London*, Fisher and Co. 1908.

Rev. A.H. Johnson, *The History of the Worshipful Company of the Drapers of London*, Oxford Clarendon Press, 1914.

(Ed.) Richard Sharpe, *Calendar of Wills Proved and Enrolled in the Court of Husting, London AD 1258-1688*, 1889.

MCA John Watney FSA. *Some account of the Hospital of St. Thomas of Acon in the Cheap, London and of the Plate of the Mercers' Company,* 1892 (first edition) 1906 (second edition).

MCA Papers relating to the Elis David Charity
MCA 1/23/1 - 1/23/37. MS.

CLSLA Parish Registers of St. John the Baptist, Croydon.

Manor of Croydon. *Minute Book of the Homage Jury 1582-1868* Transcribed by Clarence G. Paget 1928.

Parish of Croydon *Vestry Minutes* 1741-1899 (six vols.). MS.

Croydon Chronicle from 1855.

Croydon Advertiser from 1869.

Croydon Guardian from 1877.

Notebooks of Clarence G. Paget 1-20.

Plan of Stockenden Farm 1722/1755.

Lecture notes of Kenneth Ryde MS fS70(9)RYD.

Collections relating to Henry Smith Esq.

Some time Alderman of London. Nichols 1800.

LPL MS 1129 State of the Charities 1721.

(Ed.) H.C. Maxwell Lute. *Calendar of Patent Rolls*, Mackie.1908.

Vols 1-5.

SRO Correspendence and Diaries of Augustus John Hervey RN third

Earl of Bristol 1743-1779 941/50

Family Letters 1706-1904 941/70/29.

TNA MS. C 12/431/36 Mary Nesbitt's house.

CHC Report of the Commissioners for Inquiring Concerning Charities 1837 (Vol 31 P 867-871).

Scheme for Administration of the Almshouse Charity of Elis David 5 May 1893.

Scheme for Administration of the Croydon Charities of Henry Smith and Others 28 April 1893.

SELECT BIBLIOGRAPHY

N. Alvey, *From Chantry to Oxfam: A short History of Charity and Charity Legislation,* Phillimore, 1995.

J.C. Anderson, *A Short Chronicle Concerning the Parish of Croydon,* Reeves and Turner, 1882.

J.C. Anderson, *Monuments and Antiquities of Croydon Church,* 1855.

F.R.H. Du Boulay, *The Lordship of Canterbury,* Nelson, 1966.

A. Constable and Co., *The Victoria County History of Surrey,* Butler and Tanner, 1902.

J. Coulter, *Norwood Past,* Historical Publications, 1996.

Dr. Ducarel, *Some Account of the Town, Church and Archiepiscopal Palace of Croydon, in the County of Surrey, from its foundation to the year 1783.* J. Nichols, 1783.

J. Gadsby, *Village Histories: Sanderstead,* Bourne Society, 1998.

Rev. D.W. Garrow, *History and Antiquities of Croydon,* Croydon, 1818.

J. Gent, *Croydon Old and New,* Croydon Natural History and Scientific Society, 1995.

J. Gent, *Croydon Past,* Phillimore 2002.

R.A. Griffiths, *The Reign of King Henry VI,* Sutton Publishing, 1981.

A. Higham (Ed.), *Village Histories: Purley,* Bourne Society 1996.

M. Holmes, *Augustus Hervey A Naval Casanova,* Pentland Press, 1996

B. Howson, *Houses of Noble Poverty:A History of the English Almshouse,* Bellvue Books, 1993.

J. Imray, *The Charity of Richard Whittington,* Athlone Press, 1968.

J.J. Jacques, *Henry Smith and Smith's Charity,*
Surrey History Vol. IV No 5. pp259-261. 1993.

Graham and Martin, *Bermondsey Abbey,* British Archealogical Association, 1926.

L. Munby, *How Much is it Worth,* Phillimore, 1996.

E. Overton, *A Guide to the Medieval Manor,* Local History Publications, 1994.

C.G. Paget, *The Parish (Church) of Croydon.* Typescript.CLSLA.
C. G. Paget, *By-Ways in the History of Croydon,* Croydon, 1929; and *Croydon Homes of the Past,* Croydon, 1937.

J. Stow, *A Survey of London Written in the year 1598,* Sutton Publishing, 1994.

J. Ward, *Croydon in the Past,* Croydon Advertiser, 1883.

Y. Walker, *Lords of Croydon Palace,* AMCD Publishers, 1990.